My Journey
Through the
Nation of Islam

A Memoir

My Journey Through The Nation of Islam: A Memoir

The author may be contacted at

Published in the United States by Book Power Publishing,
an imprint of Niyah Press, Detroit, Michigan.
www.bookpowerpublishing.com

Book Power Publishing books may be purchased for educational, business, or sales promotional use. Special editions or book excerpts can also be created to specification. For details, contact support@bookpowerpublishing.com

First Edition

PRINTED IN THE UNITED STATES OF AMERICA.

ISBN: 978-1-945873-45-4

CONTENTS

MY JOURNEY
THROUGH THE
NATION OF ISLAM

A Memoir

LYNICE MUHAMMAD

BOOK
POWER
PUBLISHING
Detroit, Michigan

DEDICATION

This book is dedicated to the memory of the Early Pioneers, among them Elijah Poole and Clara Evans Poole. They had the vision and courage to follow the teachings of Master Fard Muhammad as a means of relieving the suffering of the so-called Negro in 1930s America. The book is also dedicated to the memory of the Later Pioneers, among them my parents. They had the vision and courage to follow the teachings of Honorable Elijah Muhammad and Mother Clara Muhammad (formerly the Pooles) as a means of relieving the suffering of the so-called Negro in 1950s America. The book is primarily and particularly dedicated to the memory of Suleiman Bilal and Muhsinah Irene Bilal, my parents, "Mama" (Irene Pacely, and then Irene X) and "Dad" (James E. Robinson, and then James E. 5x). As they journeyed through the Nation of Islam, they raised a family of eleven children with love and discipline, teaching us to treat others as we would have them treat us.

ACKNOWLEDGMENTS

First and foremost, I am grateful to Almighty G-d for inspiring me to write this book. While the writing has been a labor of love, the labor has not been easy for me, an inexperienced writer. Starting, sustaining, and completing the task would not have been possible without the aid of three people in particular: Marjorie Cowan, Faridah Pasha, and my sister Renee Hasan. They have been beta readers, and have stood by me throughout the entire process, offering suggestions and much needed encouragement. I have had professional support from Zarinah El-Amin and the sisters of the Power Author Academy run by Book Power Publishing, support for which I am most grateful. I am also grateful to Naim AbdurRafi for the many hours he devoted to finding problems and offering suggestions for strengthening the manuscript.

PREFACE

This humble contribution to the legacy of my family and that of the Nation of Islam has taken me thirteen years to complete. For the accomplishment I am grateful to G-d. I pray the result of my effort is pleasing to Him.

The impetus for my effort was a project undertaken by Sister Akanke Rasheed in 2008. The impetus for her project was an experience she had shortly before becoming a Muslim in the early nineties. At the Atlanta Masjid she questioned brothers and sisters about their paths to Islam. She was on her way to becoming a Muslim. She was curious.

She found particular relish for her questioning among older African Americans. These people were introduced to Islam through their membership in the Nation of Islam, led by its founder Elijah Muhammad. They were now practicing an Islam more recognizable as such by Muslims worldwide. They were quick, however, to credit their Nation of Islam experience for much that made applying the precepts of the Qur'an to their lives easy and enjoyable. And they were anxious for this to be known widely.

They were talking to the right person. Not only was Akanke soon to become Sister Akanke, but she was also soon to become a television producer. What she was hearing had great potential as content. The responses to her questions planted a seed. Germination would take some time.

Germination entailed Sister Akanke settling into her Islam. It also entailed her learning more about Nation of Islam and sorting through various narratives about it, the most popular being about the difference (or alleged difference) between the Nation and so-called orthodox Islam. "Nothing before it is due. Everything in G-d's time."

It was in 2008 at the Atlanta Masjid that I met Sister Akanke. She was recording interviews of Muslims whose Islamic journey had begun in the Nation of Islam, recordings which were to be broadcasted via various media. She and I talked at length. I told her about my having been raised by parents who joined the Nation of Islam when I was four years old. Her response was that I was under obligation to do a book. The seed was planted. Germination would take some time.

At some point, I am not sure when, I started to seriously consider a memoir. I began to focus thought on my Islamic journey. I began to focus thought on my growing up in the Nation of Islam. I talked with others who had been members of the Nation, some who, like me, had started out as children. I began keeping a notebook. The more I thought and talked, the faster the notebook filled up.

One discussion in particular moved things along substantially. It was an interview I gave to Sister Zaynab Ansari who was studying at Georgia State University and doing her masters thesis on Nation of Islam. The interview was videoed and shared to YouTube. My siblings saw the video. A family buzz ensued. I got a lot of feedback, a lot of information. My notebook began to really fill up.

Retirement from elementary school teaching came. It was time to put pen to paper. I got another push at the Lou Walker Senior Center in Stone Mountain, Georgia. There was a writing class, which I joined. The instructor had us reading, writing, and talking to each other about our writing. My memoir began to take shape. I joined the class in 2017 and stayed with it until Covid-19 shut us down in 2020.

INTRODUCTION

"Lynice, James, Jonathan, Renee, it's time to get up!" That was Mama waking us. She was our alarm clock. I knew I had to hit the floor. I took a nice long stretch before pulling myself out of bed. Then the aroma of coffee hit me; Maxwell House, it was Dad's favorite coffee. Mama had been up long enough to brew Dad's coffee, fix him some breakfast, and pack his lunch. Dad carried one of those classic Stanley black metal lunch boxes. There was a thermos of coffee, two sandwiches, most likely a peanut butter sandwich, and a bologna or salami sandwich. Dad sipped his coffee, ate whatever Mama had prepared for him, and he was out the door. By the time we'd washed up and made our way to the kitchen, Dad was long gone in his little red truck, pulling a yellow cement mixer.

This is a snapshot of my family in 1954. I was 7, the oldest of four. By this time my parents had been members of the Nation of Islam for three years. My father joined in 1951, at Temple No. 1, shortly after the family relocated from Bessemer, Alabama, to Detroit. My mother joined in late 1951 or early 1952. The snapshot is of a time when at least four of us children attended the University of Islam at Temple No. 1.

We had moved from Detroit into our own home in Inkster, Michigan. My family had a trusted relationship with Malcolm X. Dad was well acquainted with his brothers, Wilfred X Little and Philbert

Omar. When Malcolm was released from prison in 1952, it was from what was then the Federal Penitentiary in Milan, Michigan. He moved to Inkster and lived with his brother Wilfred. We lived within walking distance of Wilfred, and Malcolm was a frequent visitor.

At 19, I married a Muslim Minister and moved to Jackson, Mississippi. We had three children, one of whom died within days of his birth. At 25 I was a divorcee, raising two children on my own.

The marriage and breakup were a trial for me and my parents. And my parents have had their own trials. And my siblings have had their trials. But throughout all times of trial and test we all have had the comfort of the Nation of Islam, its teachings, and the sincere love of the believers. Most of all we have had our faith and trust in Almighty G-d.

CHAPTER ONE

ALABAMA TO DETROIT

I have many fond childhood memories of my mother. This is one. The year was 1950. I was barely three years old. I lived with my parents and two little brothers in Bessemer, Alabama. I was in our sandbox with my neighbor Rodger Russell. We were filling containers with sand, seeing who could fill theirs fastest. Suddenly I felt very itchy. I screamed for my mother. I knew she was somewhere nearby. Rodger was puzzled. He probably was wondering if he had done something wrong. All I knew was that I no longer wanted to be in that sandbox. I needed my mother. Mama came running out of the house. I told her about the itching. She began examining my arms, legs, and thighs. She took me out of the sandbox and sent Rodger home. We went inside, and she began drawing bathwater. She got me out of my clothes and put me into the bathtub. I did not understand what was going on, but I did not question her. Eventually I learned that red ants had invaded the sandbox. When I think about my mother and the care she gave her children, this incident comes to mind.

I am the oldest of eleven. In 1950 there were three of us, but I was the only one old enough to travel with Mama without being a bother. She took me to Sunday school while she attended church.

Sunday school for me was the church nursery. There were games with new friends. And there were songs: "Jesus Loves Me This I Know"; "He's Got the Whole World in His Hand."

The most fun came after church service. The children in the nursery would get a special treat. For me, the best treat was an ice cream cone with my favorite flavor, vanilla. I remember walking home with Mama as I enjoyed my cone.

During this time, my father worked in the coal mines in Birmingham. His decision to leave the coal mines was perhaps one of the best decisions he ever made. There were few harder and more dangerous jobs than coal mining. Dad had witnessed many miners get hurt or become ill from constantly inhaling coal dust. He saw co-workers die at an early age.

He decided to leave coal mining, but what about his wife and three children? How would he replace his coal miner salary? Alabama offered no answer to that question for a black man in the 1950s. We would have to leave Alabama.

Dad was not afraid of taking on responsibility. As a teenager he had been the man of the house, working to provide for his mother, brother, and three sisters. All who knew him knew him as a very responsible and capable person. Mama and members of her family saw Dad as a uniquely responsible black man. When he and Mama married, he moved his new bride into a completely furnished home.

Because of my father's track record, my mother trusted his decision and was willing to make the sacrifice of starting over in a new environment. Dad decided we would move to Detroit, Michigan, a destination for many who had decided as he had. Mama knew nothing about Detroit, but she supported the move with no hesitation. In the summer of 1950 Dad went to Detroit to look for a job and housing. After being away a few weeks, Dad called Mama to tell her he had found a short-term job. And he had met a Christian family living on the east side of Detroit who would rent him living space in their basement. Mama immediately prepared leave.

Late summer or early fall of 1950 we left Bessemer for Detroit. Dad had arranged with his cousin Sonny for him to drive us. Mom said her special prayers, gave her goodbyes, and we were on the road for the long ride to Detroit, Michigan. Mama and my infant brother Jonathan were in the front with Cousin Sonny. My brother James and I sat in the back with Cousin Sonny's friend.

After some time, we came to a rest stop. All the passengers in the back had been comfortably sleeping—or so we thought. My brother James may have been sleeping, but he was not comfortable. His small body had slid through a space between the backrest and the seat. He was on the floor of the body of the car, behind the back seat. He was crying, struggling without success to climb out. Cousin Sonny's friend tried to free him. He could not. Cousin Sonny joined him in the effort. The two of them could not free James. They tried going through the trunk of the car. They could not free James. By this time, I was up front with Mama. She passed me the baby and went outside to help the men. She started by supervising since their movements needed to be coordinated. At the same time, she was saying things to comfort her frightened son. Finally, she took over. I heard her praying, straining, and saying things to comfort James. I heard her shout, "Praise G-d." She had accomplished by herself what the two men could not do together. She had freed her son.

James was still crying, but he was very happy. I was very happy. Cousin Sonny and his friend were greatly relieved. We made the rest of the trip with both my brothers in the front, James sitting next to Mama, Jonathan on her lap.

If Mama was one to complain, what she encountered when we arrived in Detroit gave her something to complain about. The basement accommodations were so unappealing that our landlords were compelled to apologize. But it was what G-d had provided. It was a 'make do' situation, and Mama made do.

She made do, but her efforts were not completely successful. We were up against a Detroit winter, living in a cold and damp basement. Mama tried to protect us with extra clothing and tonics but to no avail. Jonathan, the baby, came down with pneumonia and was hospitalized for more than a week. Over the course of the winter everyone in the family was ill at some point. But we survived. Mama never complained. And she became pregnant with my first sister, Renee, who was born in June 1951.

It was probably in the spring of 1951 that my mother found a congregation of her Bessemer church, the Church of God in Christ. She probably had been directed to her new church by someone in the Bessemer congregation. In any event she started attending church, taking me with her. Dad would take care of my brothers. Dad was not a churchgoer. He was unclear about religion. You might say he was agnostic. He could not reconcile the claim that G-d was loving and just with the treatment black people got at the hands of whites. For the same reason he had a problem with the role a blonde, blue-eyed Jesus played in lives of Christians like Mama. But none of this detracted from his love for Mama. In fact, there was a time when he did attend church in Bessemer. This was before he and Mama married. He became a churchgoer long enough to impress her.

At about the time Mama was reconnecting with her church, Dad started having discussions at work and on the street with members of the Nation of Islam. Nation members were very active in reaching out and teaching on the streets of Detroit. Dad brought home copies of the *Pittsburgh Courier* and the *Amsterdam News*, two black national newspapers that carried articles by Honorable Elijah Muhammad. The articles were titled "Muhammad Speaks," which became the title of the Nation of Islam newspaper launched shortly after this time. Dad accepted an invitation to attend a meeting at Temple No. 1. He was very impressed with what he saw and heard. He began attending meetings as often as time permitted.

What he heard appealed to him because it made sense. But what he saw appealed to him even more. He saw the Fruit of Islam (FOI), black men in uniform or uniformly and neatly dressed. He saw what he considered true black manhood. He saw black brotherhood. He saw black men treating each other with respect—not cursing, threatening, or ridiculing each other. He saw black men organized to stand up for themselves. He saw an organization dedicated to protecting women and maintaining strong families. Dad had grown up in family without a father, a family that had problems because there was no man in the house. What he saw touched him deeply.

Despite growing up in a dysfunctional situation, or maybe because of it, Dad had developed very positive values. He now saw those values exemplified by an entire organization of black people. He decided to join the Nation of Islam. He wanted to be a part of the brotherhood of the Fruit of Islam.

After several attempts, his Acceptance Letter passed the scrutiny of the NOI secretary. He had written a properly formatted letter, neat in appearance, that was free of grammatical errors, in which he clearly expressed his intentions concerning the Nation of Islam. He was admitted to the fold at Temple No. 1, then housed on Frederick Street.

Dad worked at his employment for long hard hours. Still, he made sure he attended temple meetings at least once a week. As a new initiate there were things he was required to learn, that he was anxious to learn, the "Lessons": Lesson Number One; Lesson Number Two; Student Enrollment; The Actual Facts. Mastering the information contained in the lessons was part of the process of becoming a full-fledged member, becoming a brother with a Muslim name, one who has received his 'X.'

Significant in the process was reaching and sustaining a sales quota, selling Muhammad Speaks. This was a real challenge for Dad because of his long and hard employment hours, but he eventually got the hang of it. After a few months he earned his 'X.' He became a fully registered member of the Nation of Islam, with the name James E. 5X. Dad was thirty at the time. It was a proud moment.

There is an oft repeated family story, one that came into being by both Mama and Dad sharing it at one time or another. The story captures the tension of that time when Dad was a new NOI member and Mama was still very much a Christian. Jonathan, James, and I were sitting at the breakfast table where Mama was serving us what she felt was a good Saturday morning breakfast. She had prepared bacon, eggs, and grits. Just as we finished blessing the table and were beginning to eat, Dad suddenly began removing the bacon from the plates and throwing it into the garbage. Mama was startled. She was very confused as to why Dad would put good food into the trash. She was sure Dad had taken leave of his senses. My brothers and I were surprised at what we saw. Dad said he did not want his children to be fed any pork. He went on about hog meat not being suitable for human consumption. That pork meat had trichina worms. Further, he said, the Bible and the Qur'an speak against eating pork. That the reason the hog was created was to eat garbage and filth. He wanted us to eat only chicken, beef, and fish. After he finished talking, Mama asked if we could just finish what was on our plates? Dad shook his head. "No way." Mom just couldn't understand. Dad began to look around the house, and a picture on the wall caught his eye. It was a classic portrait of Jesus. He took the picture and turned it over and, looking at me, said that I should not believe that Jesus was a blue-eyed, blonde-haired man. "No, Jesus looked more like you and me. He had kinky hair and olive-colored skin."

Mama was a devout Christian. In Bessemer she had taught Sunday school. She was well read in Scripture. At her new church in Detroit, she taught Sunday school. Dad and Mama agreed that James and I would alternately attend church with Mama and temple meetings with Dad. Being a perceptive child, I was aware of the tension in the home, and I was happy to be a part of some resolution. I don't remember much about temple meetings at this point, but Sunday school with Mama was the treat it had been for me back in Bessemer. I enjoyed the Bible stories. I especially enjoyed the delicious food.

During this time Mama was pregnant. In June my first sister, Renee, was born. At Herman Kieffer Hospital. Maybe it was in the fall that Mama began getting visits from sisters of the NOI temple. Eventually she accepted an invitation to attend a temple meeting.

Mama was impressed. She was impressed with what she learned, especially about health and food preparation. She was impressed with the sisters, their confidence, their compassion, their dignified attire. Just as Dad had envisioned himself a member of FOI, Mama began to see her place among the sisters. It wasn't long before Mama became Sister Irene. Of course, Dad was happy. But I am not sure he was happier than me, a four-year-old child. Complete peace had descended upon our home. All praise is due to G-d.

CHAPTER TWO

INKSTER, MICHIGAN

In 1952 we moved to Inkster, Michigan, into a new home. The house was very modest, with only two bedrooms and a bath on the first floor and unfinished space on the second floor, enough for a few more rooms. Dad had worked very hard to make this happen and, of course, Mama had supported him any way she could.

The City of Inkster, population of around twenty-five thousand in 2010, was officially a village when we moved there, with a population of around sixteen thousand. Incorporation as a city did not come until 1964. Today Inkster is considered a suburb of Detroit. When we moved there it was not the suburbs. Inkster was a rural hamlet. Many people kept cows, goats, sheep, pigs, and chickens. We did not have any animals, but Dad always had a small garden. Having a garden was essential since major food shopping meant travelling at least a few miles, to places like Garden City, Westland, Ypsilanti, Dearborn Heights, Lincoln Park, or Romulus.

There were ditches everywhere. Paved streets were rare. Our house, 4151 Henry Street, was on an unpaved cul de sac (i.e., "dead-in street") separated by a fence from Douglas Elementary School. It was an ideal street for children since there was no through traffic.

Inkster was largely a black residential community. During the twenties and thirties, Black Americans who had migrated from the South to Detroit found work at the Ford plant in Dearborn. The trip from Dearborn to Inkster was much shorter than the trip to Detroit. So, they began settling in Inkster. Blacks were not allowed to reside in Dearborn.

The racism of Dearborn was reflective of most of America at the time. In fact, Dearborn outdid most similar northern cities with respect to racism. "Keep Dearborn Clean," the city's motto, was interpreted by all black people to mean the city wished not to be defiled by the presence of black people as residents. "If you have work here, fine. Do your work and leave."

Orville Liscum Hubbard was the mayor of Dearborn for thirty-six years, from 1942 to 1978. Throughout his tenure he promoted segregationist policies. But he insisted his segregationist stance should not be attributed to racism. "I'm not a racist, but I just hate those black bastards." Out of concern that the 1967 Detroit riots (aka "Detroit Rebellion") might spill over into Dearborn, His Honor instructed his police force to shoot looters on sight. Effectively, this meant that a black person on any street in Dearborn during this period could be shot, regardless of his or her reason for being there.

Before we left Detroit, Dad set his sights on learning all he could about building manholes, catch basins, and sumps. There was a building boom in Detroit, so construction of these facilities was in great demand. The temporary jobs Dad took usually were in this kind of construction. Sometimes he would take a menial position not directly involved in actual construction, or even volunteer to do errands, just so he could be on a job site where he could learn by observing or filling in.

Soon after moving to Inkster, Dad formed a construction company. The building being done in Detroit by the Public Lighting Commission created a demand for manholes, catch basins, sumps, and sewers. Loans from brothers at Temple No. 1 helped him get started. We were all very proud to see Dad taking off in the morning in his little red truck pulling a cement mixer. He was able to give employment to temple brothers. Initially Mama was his bookkeeper. When James and Jonathan reached their teens, they joined Dad in the business, learning from him masonry and other required skills. Eventually the company took on the name "Three Brothers Construction Company." The name pays homage to the brothers who helped Dad get started with their loans. There are many homes and industrial buildings in Detroit that have been provisioned with the facilities built by Three Brothers Construction Company.

One of our neighbors was Wilfred X. Little, the brother of Malcolm X (Little). Malcolm's initial imprisonment had been in Massachusetts. Toward the end of his sentence, he was transferred to Milan Penitentiary in Michigan. His release address was the home of his brother Wilfred.

Malcolm needed a job. Dad was anxious to help him. Malcolm was willing to do the hard work performed by Dad's company, but he was not built physically for digging manholes and the rest. He tried, but without good results for either him or Dad. So, Dad assigned him to flagging, and that worked, but something better came along.

Mama was the source of that something better. She had become a direct selling representative for Stanley Home Products. She did demonstrations in our home and in the homes of prospects. Dad and Mama invited Malcolm to a presentation. Selling! This was for Malcolm. Selling, but of an entirely different kind, is what he did before going to prison. He caught on quickly. He shadowed Mama for a while. In fact, Mama even got requests from women that she allow her handsome young protégé to do the demonstration. Before long Malcolm was a representative, out on his own building a clientele and attracting others to become representatives.

Malcolm was a successful Stanley Home Products representative for several months. This career ended when, through the efforts of his brothers Wilfred and Philbert Omar, Malcolm began teaching at Temple No. 1. From there he became Assistant Minister Malcolm. The rest is well-known history.

Brother Wilfred was one of just a few members of Temple No. 1 who lived in Inkster. Another was Brother Norris, our letter carrier. Everyone traveled to Detroit for weekly meetings at the temple, but the Inkster brothers also met regularly at our house. They brought friends and neighbors to these meetings for the purpose of introducing them to the Nation. Sometimes our little living room would be filled with what seemed like fifteen people. Of course, Mama gladly assumed the role of gracious hostess by serving tea and treats.

To the extent that her many duties would allow, Mama became fully involved in the activities for sisters at the temple. She became expert at baking the whole wheat bread and bean pies for which the Nation has become known. The navy bean soup also became a staple of our diets.

It was not long before Mama became truly expert at baking. You could even say she developed skill that was legendary. Certainly, her ability became well known and much appreciated on our little street. At least once a month she would do a major baking. It was for the family, but she knew neighbors would just happen to show up having the expectation that hospitality would be extended in the form of some fresh hot buttered bread and maybe even some blueberry pie.

I remember those days well because I was directly involved. I was the oldest of what became a family of seven children while we were in Inkster. I was always busy helping Mama. We would get started shortly after Dad left for work, between 6:30 and 7. I can hear her giving me instructions: "Lynn," she would call out, "I need you to take out some honey, 1/2 cup of lukewarm water for the three packages of Fleischmann's Yeast, salt, sugar, wheat and white flour, four large eggs, and Mazola Oil."

Eventually the smell of fresh bread would permeate the air of the entire block and sometimes even further. I recall once returning from school on the school bus and getting an aroma suggesting we were near a bakery. There was no bakery. It was my house. And the bus was at least a mile from the house. I have many fond memories of Mama's baking.

The annual Savior's Day Convention is another fond memory. It was an exhilarating experience for the many reasons a child would find it so. And it was an exhilarating experience for me as I entered my teen years and was developing an understanding of the Nation. Honorable Elijah Muhammad's followers would come together to celebrate accomplishments made in the previous year. It was a time to update everyone about the Nation's affairs. It was a time to interact with other believers, socialize, enjoy good food, and enjoy each other's company.

The drive for us from Inkster was almost four hours. The Friday before the event, Dad would take off from work. Mama would prepare a picnic basket filled with delightful things to eat. She would have fried chicken and potato salad, lemonade (Dad's favorite), fruits, chips, cookies, and a big chocolate cake! Sometimes we'd stay at a hotel for two days, or with relatives, or sometimes we would bunk with other Muslims who invited us to their homes. Mama would always pack blankets in case we needed to make pallets.

The Savior's Day Convention was filled with positive energy. It was the energy of the meetings at Temple No. 1 magnified and multiplied. The energy of temple meetings was the energy of my home magnified and multiplied. I look back and realize that my siblings and I were very fortunate. We were surrounded by esteem building positive energy. We were part of a positive and forward-thinking organization. We had positive and forward-thinking parents who loved each other and loved us. Our surroundings in Inkster were friendly and safe—due in part to the fence at the end of the street separating us from the school grounds.

We were equipped to deal with unpleasant realities we encountered outside our positive, friendly, and safe circumference. Of course, Dearborn would be a place where we would be exposed to an unpleasant reality, the reality of racism in America. Mama did something not many blacks would attempt during the 1950s. She took her five children to the Dearborn Library. At the time, there were five of us, so that would have been James, Jonathan, Renee, Obadiah, and me. I recall the strange looks we got on the bus, not to mention the looks we received upon entering the library.

The librarian tried her best to dissuade Mama from library visits. She told us we did not have proper identification. She needed copies of birth certificates, Social Security cards, and other forms of identification. She did not realize the resolve of my mother.

We returned within a week with the documents requested. The librarian had no reason to deny our right to check out books. However, she pretended she was doing Mama a favor by allowing one book per child. Of course, Mama chose as many as she liked, in addition to some 331/3 records.

Library trips were very special for us. We were getting out of the house and going someplace. And we were reading and learning new things. We made sure we were on our best behavior. The librarian commented on how well-behaved we were.

Mama told us we were to take good care of the books. We would not eat anything while reading them, and we would pay particular attention not to soil or tear the books but enjoy and share them. Mama turned an unpleasant reality into something very pleasant and very positive for her children.

CHAPTER THREE

WHITE CLOUDS, MICHIGAN

In the spring of 1953, our family had the opportunity to live in White Clouds, Michigan. The reason for our temporary stay there was that Honorable Elijah Muhammad had requested FOI to take part in a nation-building effort. The nation-building effort was a call for followers to invest in farmland and develop it.

The Honorable Elijah Muhammad had invested in farmland in White Clouds, Michigan, and later in many other cities.

My father shared with brothers at the temple that he had attended college at Tuskegee Institute, in Alabama. His concentration was Agricultural Engineering. Before marrying my mother, he'd completed enough of the two-year program to acquire practical experience and know-how. The program had prepared him with skills to operate a farm. Because of his preparation, the brothers suggested he organize and lead the workforce for the farm in White Clouds. Knowing what to plant in a particular season, he would be able to accomplish what Honorable Elijah Muhammad was encouraging his followers to do— take farmland, make it productive, live on it, and thrive on it.

Honorable Elijah Muhammad purchased the land in White Clouds with the idea of having a group of brothers work the land

and make it productive. He wanted to establish it as a model for the rest of the Nation. However, it came down to my father being the only one who was able to or willing to make the sacrifice. My father ended up taking his family to Whites Clouds, to the farm. The purchase of this property in the '50s was a continuation of a process that began in the '40s while Honorable Elijah Muhammad was in prison. A copy of the deed of purchase is in the Nation of Islam's archives.

The farm already had a small farmhouse with a frame that was on bricks. The property needed some attention for it to be habitable. The first step was to make it livable for a small family of three or four people. In retrospect, before making the house available, it should have been bricked entirely. There should have been a line run to the house to add a bathroom. Outside of the house, several feet away was a barn that housed three cows. There was a Jersey, Holstein, a black cow, and a bull. Also, there was a wired chicken coup, with quite a few chickens known to lay lots of fresh eggs. There was also a tool shed that housed many needed tools and supplies. The tool shed was also someplace where the three ducks frequented, along with four sheep. Also housed was a coupler tractor, a plow, and many hand tools.

The place had the look and feel of someone having built it very hastily. In the kitchen was an icebox instead of a refrigerator. There was a small table and a few chairs. Also, there was an old-fashioned coal-burning stove in the corner of the floor. Mama burned wood. There was an old-fashioned oven mom rarely used. There was little cabinet space in the kitchen. There were two small cabinets and space for a sink—but no sink. There was no running water in the house. Mama transported water from the well in an aluminum hand bucket that she kept on the stove for cooking. She used a larger bucket when transporting water for bathing and washing clothes.

There was a living room. Between the living room and the kitchen were two small rooms. The first room was a sitting room. Renee and I used it as our bedroom. Mama and Dad use the other room as their bedroom. James and Jonathan slept on the floor or on the couch in the living room.

One of the enjoyable things about the farm was that I could pick fresh fruit from the orchard or eat cucumbers and radishes fresh from the garden. Mama would gather fresh vegetables to cook for dinner each day. Dad was out all day in the field, planting or harvesting. I enjoyed the big juicy cucumbers, the okra, green beans, tomatoes, corn, such a variety of good fresh vegetables. We always had something new from which to choose. We had chickens. Whenever Mama wanted to prepare chicken for dinner; she only had to cut off the heads of one or two chickens, pluck the feathers, and cook the chickens.

There was an old phonogram in the corner of the living room that looked like something from the Roaring Twenties. When I asked Mama what it was, she explained that it played records and that you could listen and dance to the music. From time to time, Mama would let me listen to it. However, there was not anything that interested me. So basically, it just sat there collecting dust.

I enjoyed helping my father with milking the cows and thought it was exciting. I remember waking up early one morning excited to join Dad. He promised I could assist him with milking the cows. We walked across the yard to the barn where the cows and bull were housed. I was puzzled by the first thing my father did. He tied the tail of the cow into a knot. He then placed the bucket under the cow's udder. I asked why he had tied the cow's tail? Dad explained that cows tend to swing their tails during milking, sometimes causing milk to spill. Tying also prevented the cow from hitting Dad with its tail. Dad filled the small bucket first, as he finished milking one cow, and poured the milk into a larger bucket.

As Dad milked the cows, since he had done this so many times, he had a rhythm to how he grabbed, pulled, and squeezed the teats so milk would flow into his bucket. Dad saw how excited I was about the process, so he allowed me to try. My small hands were so weak he had to assist me with squeezing the milk from the cow's teats. It felt good to be able to do at least a couple of squeezes. The cows were very productive. My father would take milk to the diary daily, where much of it was made into butter, cream, and cheese.

There was something I did not like during our stay in White Clouds. It was the outhouse, which was where we'd go to relieve ourselves. Mama would keep a potty in the house for night use. I resented, no I outright hated going to the outhouse! I shared with Dad what I was feeling. Dad came up with an idea. He said he would dig a couple of holes that I could do my business in if I promised I would cover them up with dirt after finishing. Dad dug the holes in an area that was away and out of sight of everything. At least we thought it was out of sight. My brothers would sometimes discover what I was up to. They were curious and would not allow me any peace or privacy.

Mom had activities I could do in the house, but I preferred being outside. There was always such a freshness about being outside. I felt carefree and happy. For the most part, living on the farm in White Clouds was an adventure for me. There were three ducks we named BOBO, RINSO BLUE, CEDRIC, and we used to have fun chasing them around the shed and out into the yard.

I enjoyed Mama's breakfasts. She would sometimes cook pheasant or smelts in a deep fryer. She would also make pancakes from scratch. My Dad enjoyed her pancakes with lots of butter and Alaga syrup, or if she did not make pancakes, she would make the best melt-in-your mouth buttermilk biscuits.

Our family moved from Inkster to White Clouds to honor my parents' commitment to the Honorable Elijah Muhammad. He wanted to see what kind of yields could be produced. My father worked hard from the early spring until fall, trying to do what Honorable Elijah Muhammad instructed him to do. However, my father was the only one who followed through on his word. We were taught in the Nation of Islam, "My word is my Bond, and my Bond is my Life, and I shall give my Life before my Word shall Fail." Obviously, for others, it was just lip service.

There was one brother who did come to assist my father a couple of times.

This was Brother Willard. He assisted Dad for two weekends in a row. He helped him do the initial planting. I could be wrong, but I do not recall any other brothers coming to White Clouds. Despite this, my father planted an excellent crop. After a few months, Dad's beautiful green vegetables and fruits were ripe and plentiful. It must have been during the early spring when we left Inkster for White Clouds. I remember Mama saying I had missed equivalent to three months of school.

Dad made several trips to Chicago, to report directly to Honorable Elijah Muhammad. Once, Honorable Elijah Muhammad asked Dad to allow my brothers James and Jonathan to spend the night in his home. Dad said he would have, except that he knew the boys sometimes had "accidents." My brothers were still four and five. Because my father did not want to be embarrassed, nor have my brothers embarrassed, he declined the offer told honorable Elijah Muhammad he and the boys were appreciative.

Dad had planted green beans, lots of tomatoes, corn, turnip greens, okra, squash, and potatoes. I know he had radishes. I liked the radishes straight from the garden, the crunchy, tingly taste of them. There was so much good stuff. It was just a wonderful experience for my brothers and me. Years later I realized the experience was not as wonderful for Mama and Dad. It was time of great sacrifice.

It was not easy for Mama because she would have to go to the well to draw water to wash clothes, cook, and get water to use for washing dishes, bathing, or washing clothes. Whatever she did, she would have to go to the well and pump water. I'm sure this was a strain on her. There were none of the conveniences we had become accustomed to in Inkster. And she was four or five months pregnant.

Because she loved my father and my father had made a commitment to Honorable Elijah Muhammad, my mother stood by him. Now looking back as an adult, I know it was a very hard task for my father because he didn't have much more than the essential equipment to work with. There was a tractor someone had purchased for the farm, basic tools, and plows. Fortunately, water was not an issue. The Nation had made an arrangement with a neighboring farmer whereby we always had water sufficient for crop irrigation and watering the animals.

If I had to say what was the best part of being on the farm for me those few months, it would be the freedom to run around and be exposed to so much space, the fresh air, the tasty clean water, and the fresh smell of nature. We could eat fresh fruits and vegetables all the time. The water that came from the well was always fresh and clean. The only thing was that you'd have to go and pump it. Basically, it was on Mama to pump the water.

I appreciate the fact, one I learned when I grew up, that the only way we were able to make it during that time was that my father used his ingenuity to barter and sell the fruits, vegetables, and other things the farm produced. He would go to an air open market. People were very happy to get fresh produce. Thanks to Allah, with the money Dad was able to generate, the family was able to make it back to Inkster.

My parents did what they had to do to get back on course. This meant getting caught up with mortgage payments, utility bills, and doing things they had neglected for those six months we were gone. Mama had to go through and re-organize the house and get things back as she had left them. Dad had to get back to his construction company. While in White Clouds, the day-to-day operation of the construction company was in the hands of his brother-in-law, Johnny George. The believers in Detroit were supportive as much as they could be. They took up a collection to assist the family until we could get back to the regular routine of my father managing his construction company and Mama getting back into the groove of being a wife and homemaker at 4151 Henry Street. There was a couple that had been staying at the house, a Brother Joe and a Sister Evelina. As I recall, they were a lovely couple with two children. A daughter Mary Jo and a son Little Jo. Instead of asking them to leave, Mama and Dad allowed them to move upstairs until they could find a place to stay.

I think if you were to ask my father what the most disappointing thing about the White Clouds experience was, he would say it was the brothers not showing up to help as they had promised. Again, I can recall only one brother coming during the time we were there.

My parents operated in one accord. My father and my mother felt the same. When the call was made for willing and able helpers, they answered the call. They both were ready and willing to make the sacrifice for the good of their community. I thank Allah. I pray their effort will be recorded as a good deed for them. I thank you, Allah, for allowing me to be a witness bearer, even though I was only six years old.

Mama with her water bucket

CHAPTER FOUR

UNIVERSITY OF ISLAM

Throughout the United States there are Sister Clara Muhammad Schools attached to most mosques that grew out of Nation of Islam temples. They are grade schools that were known as University of Islam schools before temples became mosques in 1975. Then, University of Islam became Sister Clara Muhammad Schools.

Sister Clara Muhammad was the wife of Honorable Elijah Muhammad. Facing threats of punishment by the Detroit Board of Education, even being confronted at the door of her home by the police, she refused to allow her children to attend Detroit public schools. She taught them at home. Honorable Elijah Muhammad and the Detroit Board of Education came to terms. In 1934 he instituted formal grade school instruction at Temple No. 1, calling the school University of Islam.

The name 'University of Islam' speaks to many aspects of the vision of Honorable Elijah Muhammad. A central concern of his was the low self-esteem of black people. Black people of the thirties were in "bad shape." Others saw us as nothing. We, in many cases, saw ourselves as less than that. We were just three generations from slavery. That kind of thinking—especially our negative thinking about ourselves—could not advance us. It could only take us back-wards. It threatened our existence.

So, we could not be UNIA, the Universal Negro Improvement Association of Marcus Garvey. And we could not be NAACP, the National Association for the Advancement of Colored People of WEB DuBois. We were not "Negroes" and "Colored." We were not in need of "improvement" and "advancement." We simply needed to recognize and actualize our value, our G-d given high status within the human family.

So, we were not an "association." We were a NATION, the Nation of Islam. We were a people guided by principles laid down by G-d in the Quran. We were a special people, much like the Israelites of old, who were a special people guided by the principles G-d laid down in the Torah. Honorable Elijah Muhammad insisted we think beyond our status as people in "bad shape" living in the United States of America, denigrated, and even despised. No, we were citizens of the world, special beings in the cosmos belonging to Almighty G-d.

Of course, when I was in the elementary grades at UOI I knew nothing about this vision of Honorable Elijah Muhammad. What I knew is that we students felt special. We were made to feel special.

One of the highlights of my days at UOI happened when I was about ten. A teacher sent me on an errand to the "Luncheonette," the restaurant next door to the temple. Lo and behold! Who was sitting in the restaurant but Honorable Elijah Muhammad himself? My heart pounded with excitement. He immediately rose from his seat, bowed, and greeted me with "Assalaamu alaykum." I quickly composed myself and bashfully returned his greeting. He asked my name. I told him. He asked me to repeat it, and I did. He asked me if I knew the meaning of my name. I told him I did not. He took a little notebook from his pocket and wrote my name in it. He said his intention was to look it up later. To this day I vividly recall how special I felt at that moment. I look back and realize that what I was struck by was his grace, humility, and graciousness.

Something similar occurred some years earlier, another instance of adults displaying special regard for NOI children. Malcolm visited the school often. By this time, he was traveling around the country, making presentations at temples and other places. For us children he was a celebrity. We were flattered by his taking time to visit our school. On one of his early visits, he singled out my siblings and me. "Why, those are the children of Brother James E. 5X." He had visited our home in Inkster when he lived there. Maybe that's how he could recognize us. Maybe he recognized Dad's prominent facial features reflected in all of us. In any event, that was a very big moment for my siblings and me.

The name 'University of Islam' also speaks to the belief of Honorable Elijah Muhammad that childhood education should be universal from the outset. When a child is old enough for formal education, that education should not be restrictive and confining. If the child is old enough for formal education, certainly the child is old enough to explore the universe. Of course, stress must be laid on the "3 R's," (Reading, Writing, Arithmetic = "Reading, Riting, Rithmetic"), so the child has tools for exploration. However, that exploration should not be delayed until the child has facility with the upper levels of the 3R's, say grammar, writing composition, and algebra—which does not happen until middle school normally. Exploration should begin in kindergarten—and before. This is education thinking that did not become fashionable in public education until the sixties, most notably with Head Start. Honorable Elijah Muhammad and Mother Clara were way ahead of their time. It is reasonable to assume that Mother Clara, mother and teacher of her children, was the initial promoter of these views and that her husband simply followed her lead and applied her views as principles for the education of all Nation of Islam children.

The education thinking of Elijah and Clara Muhammad was in line with the Montessori Method (of the Italian educator Maria Montessori) that was then barely beginning to take hold in the United

States—and only in private schools. American public schools in the nineteen thirties were not places where real education happened for most students. Elijah and Clara Muhammad were not operating from a separatist position when they kept their children out of Detroit public schools. No, they wanted their children to be educated.

Who is the Original Man? (Answer: The Original Man is the owner, the maker, cream of the Planet Earth, god of the universe.) I can ask and answer this question today, at age seventy. I could do the same at age six. My brother James could do the same at age five. My brother Jonathan could do the same at age four. My sister, Renee, cajoled Mama into allowing her to attend UOI when she was three and some months. I am not certain she mastered these Student Enrollment questions at that time, but she did eventually.

How does this kind of rote learning have anything to do with the education of a child? I am a retired elementary teacher. I taught in a Sister Clara Muhammad school and in a public school. "EVERYTHING" is my answer. What child in a typical public elementary school is encouraged to consider his or her origin or the origin or the universe, or its dimensions?

Who is the Colored Man? (Answer: The Colored Man is the Caucasian, Yacub-made Devil, Skunk of the Planet Earth.) What is the population of the Original Nation in the wilderness of North America and all over Planet Earth? How much does the Earth weigh? By how much land are we surrounded? By how much water are we surrounded?

Again, my answer concerning the relevance of such questions to my education and that of my siblings and other classmates, is that they had everything to do with it. At ages four, five, and six we were inspired to think about ourselves relative to the people around us, the earth on which we lived, and the cosmos in which we lived.

We were inspired to become readers, and that is what we did. Neither my siblings nor I were truly proficient readers when we enrolled in UOI in late 1953, but that changed quickly. No word on a sign or billboard went unlearned by me when Mama or Dad were nearby for me to question them. And Mama relieved the teaching burden on her by taking us to the Dearborn Public Library often. Then I started conducting reading classes in a space Dad provisioned with a chalkboard upstairs in our house. James and Jonathan were especially interested in learning to read the newspaper so they could follow the sports news and read the comics. So, at school we mastered the times table and read the primers (often donated by local public schools), but we became truly educated by exploring on our own, having been inspired to explore by the facts of Student Enrollment.

And as for the 'Facts' I will say this. We found some of the facts to be true. And those we could not confirm, we also could not disprove. Moreover, these same facts were those that Mama and every sister learned in MGT/GCC, and Dad and every brother learned in FOI. Some facts they knew to be true, and those they could not confirm, they could not disprove. This had been the case for twenty years. The facts made us the Nation of Islam, a happy and confident family, a unified people.

UOI utilized a "one-room schoolhouse" concept but not to a strict degree. Not in the beginning but eventually there were three grade groupings: Kindergarten and First; Second and Third; Fourth, Fifth, and Sixth. There was no rigid separation by age, and there certainly was no ranking within grade groupings. This encouraged us children to view our education as a team effort, a Nation of Islam effort. We maintained helpful attitudes toward our classmates in class, and those who could be together out of class, like members of the same family, helped each other out of class. Teachers were very careful to identify students who needed individual attention and patiently gave them that attention.

The UOI curriculum comprised the essential areas of study found in all public schools: reading, grammar, penmanship, arithmetic, geography, and science. The school year was the entire year. There was ample time for students to do extra studying if needed for staying abreast. The school week was Monday, Wednesday, Thursday, and Friday. Tuesday was a part of the school week but not a time for classes. Teachers used Tuesdays for preparation and school administration tasks. Tuesday was a time for parents to make sure students who needed to do extra work to stay abreast did just that. For my family, Tuesday was typically the day for visiting the Dearborn Public Library.

In 1958, when I was eleven, Temple No. 1 had moved from Fredrick Street to John C. Lodge Expressway. The school had operated for three years at this location, but in 1958 the school was closed by authorities for "code violations." The school did not reopen until the 1970s when the temple moved to 11529 Linwood Avenue (where it eventually became Masjid Wali Muhammad).

When the public-school year began in September 1958, Jonathan and Renee enrolled in the elementary school in Inkster. James and I resumed our education at McMichael Junior High School in Detroit. I was only eleven, but based on academic proficiency I was admitted to the eighth grade. James, only ten at the time, was admitted to the seventh grade.

There was a period of adjustment. I had come from a school where I was one among sixty at most. At McMichael I was one among hundreds. The learning atmosphere, when it was serious—and it was not always—was about competition and rarely about mutual success. Teachers were not able to or, possibly, not inclined to truly attend to the needs of individual students. This did not pose a problem for me or James. We were able to hold our own academically for the two years we were at McMichael. It's just that the caring and supportive environment of University of Islam did not exist at McMichael. My new school was not a bad place. It just was not UOI.

McMichael was not University of Islam in another important aspect. I heard and saw things, improper things, I had never heard or saw at UOI. I learned to accept this as what I might expect from people who are lost. Associated with this was the challenge of being accepted by my classmates. It took some months. The issue was my Islamic dress, my long skirts. In fact, I even cheated a little by rolling up my waist band to shorten my skirt. Soon this became unnecessary. Mama and other mothers of girls attending public schools relaxed the rules by allowing us to shorten our skirts to calf length. Also, there were some Muslim girls from Detroit at McMichael. We supported each other.

James and I were at McMichael for two years. We both transferred at the same time. I entered the tenth grade at Inkster High School in 1960. At the same time James transferred to Fellrath Junior High School in Inkster. Five of us completed grade school at Inkster High School: Obadiah, Renee, Jonathan, James, and I. My other siblings completed their grade school educations at University of Islam when it re-opened in the seventies.

Inkster, Michigan, was ninety-seven per cent black at that time. This was reflected in the student composition of the schools. There were only two white teachers. I recall two black counselors who encouraged only the "talented tenth" of the student body to take courses that would prepare them for college. Certainly, those two counselors could have learned much from the concerned and caring educators with whom I had interacted at University of Islam. Many of those UOI teachers, by the way, worked for no pay. Those who were paid earned nowhere near the salaries of public-school teachers. I list here the names of those beautiful Muslims. Names with annotations were teachers we saw regularly. The others filled in and helped. (May Allah Almighty grant them all immense rewards):

SISTER MAMIE

Generally, Sister Mamie was our "home-room" teacher. Other teachers came in when it was time for them to teach their subjects. Sister Mamie was a "drill sergeant." Fortunately, her style of teaching was the exception and not the rule. She made a profound impression on me, someone who eventually spent thirty years as an elementary teacher, so I cannot forget her.

SISTER OZETTA

Sister Ozetta was a conscientious and committed teacher. She had been a Social Worker in Detroit's Merit System before teaching at UOI. She was patient and considerate but was known not to take any nonsense. She was strict but fair. You could tell she loved teaching. We enjoyed learning from her. She assisted each child with whatever the assignment. When we asked questions, she would stop and ponder. We valued what she shared. She taught us reading, writing, arithmetic, and penmanship. Sister Ozetta had beautiful, legible handwriting. She made sure we learned to print and write cursively. She enjoyed teaching English. She enunciated words slowly and correctly. She was determined to set a good example so we could pattern ourselves after her. She tried to give us a good background in grammar, spending much time on the parts of speech and basic writing skills. She made sure we understood the concepts she was teaching.

SISTER FERN (WHO BECAME TAUHEEDAH MAHMOUD)

Sister Tauheedah exhibited the best qualities of a good teacher. She also was an excellent example of a good wife and mother. Sister Tauheedah demonstrated all the things I wanted to be. She had a family that she was devoted to. She always took the time to say thoughtful and kind words to others. It was so impressive that she could balance home, family, and teaching. Sometimes she would leave for a month or two and come back with a new baby. The babies would be very hefty, and it was hard to believe that this little lady could have birthed these large babies. She was a very small-framed woman. I would wonder how someone as small as sister Tauheedah could produce these big babies, which she carried on her side while she taught. She would find an area to breastfeed the baby when she needed to and then come back and continue teaching. It was amazing to me, and I just admired how she could manage to do all these things. She was the mother, the wife, and the teacher. I always said I wanted to be like sister Tauheedah when I grew up.

BROTHER ERNEST

An excellent teacher. He taught math. He was very articulate and a good-natured person. We loved brother Ernest. Among students he was "Skelo" because he was very thin. He had a great sense of humor and would tell us stories that kept us entertained while we learned.

And there were: Brother Moselle, Sister Emma, Sister Irene, Brother Kyra, Sister Barbara

CHAPTER FIVE

QUEEN ZENOBIA

As it came closer to Mama's delivery time, she decided to give birth at home with the aid of a midwife instead of going to the hospital. Mama was having her baby at 4151 Henry Street.

Mother Josie Shaw was the sister others recommended to be the midwife. She had delivered many babies in the community. She was loved and respected by the young couples at Temple No.1. She was said to have tremendous resilience and patience with mothers-to-be. Mother Josie encouraged the mothers to relax as they brought forth their babies. "Don't rush the process," she would say. "They'll get here when they're ready to come."

We were very excited and hoped we would get to witness the event. Mama called Mother Josie when she felt it was time for her to deliver. Dad left to pick up Mother Josie and bring her to the house. Mother Josie had packed her bags and was ready to spend as many nights as necessary with Mama until the baby was here.

One thing we loved about Mother Josie was her spirit. She always had a smile on her face and a special way of talking. She was originally from Mississippi.

Mother Josie was about 5'2" tall. She was a round, dumpy little lady with eyes that seemed to smile whenever she spoke. She loved listening to soap operas ("stories"): Search for Tomorrow, The Edge of Night. The Guiding Light. She'd talked about the stories as though the characters were people she really knew.

Mama had kicked dad out of his room. His refuge was the chair in the corner of the living room. Even when Mama wasn't expecting, he would seek this chair out. It was one of those high back, leg extensors that were adjustable. There was a handle on the side that you could push up or down to stretch your legs. After dinner, he would find his way to his favorite chair. Dad said this was where he got his best sleep.

Mother Josie and Mama were busy with the door closed. Everyone in the house was anxiously waiting to hear something; we were waiting to hear the cry of the new baby. It took several hours of coaxing and waiting. We went to bed and awoke the next day, and nothing had occurred. Dad had gone to work, but the rest of the family, James, Jonathan, Renee, and I were anxiously waiting. About mid-morning, we heard Mama. Soon we heard the new baby cry.

Mother Josie had me bring hot water and clean towels to the door. She had everything else she needed. She said we would see Mama and the new baby once they were all cleaned up. We all had lots of questions. Mother Josie answered our queries as Mama and the new baby rested.

Mama and Dad named the new baby boy Obadiah. "Obie" was born October 12, 1953. Obadiah is the name of Mama's father and her oldest brother. Over the next couple of days, Mama and family were inundated with visitors, Muslim sisters, and family, dropping in to see the new baby, bringing gifts and food.

Mama and Dad attended the Savior's Day Convention in Chicago, in February 1954. Mama had taken time to arrange care for the five children while they were gone.

Sister Addie Mohammed and her daughter Essie were our babysitters. Everything went okay until it was time to feed baby

Obadiah. We tried everything to get him to stop crying. He cried and cried and would not drink the breast milk Mama had taken time to pump. We tried putting the milk in a baby cup, which he refused to accept. We tried feeding him a little applesauce from a cup; this too he refused to accept. Mama and Dad would be gone until Sunday night; it was Friday evening. The only thing we could get Obadiah to take was water and juice. He would pause from crying long enough to take short naps. No one got any rest until Mama and Dad returned. This was truly a trial. Obie let it be known he was displeased about Mama being gone. After my parents returned, the first order of business was for Mama to breastfeed Obadiah.

Obadiah grew up to be a very popular young man, very bright and intelligent. Since he was younger than James and Jonathan, he would find himself not included in many games and activities they participated in. He would create his own games. He was the only one of the eleven children to become proficient in music. He learned to play the clarinet while attending Fellrath high Jr. He joined the Inkster High School band. He was voted most likely to succeed when he graduated in 1969.

Mama did a repeat performance in 1955 when she gave birth to Nancy Marie. She was born May 9th, 1955. Mama again called on Mother Josie and delivered Nancy at 4151 Henry Street. Of course, sisters called to congratulate Mama and the family. Muslims and family members dropped by to check on Mama and to see the new arrival. Many brought food and gifts. Mama thought it was good to name her new baby after her mother Nancy and after Mother Clara's mother, Marie. As soon as Nancy was old enough to change her name, she did. When asked why she changed her name, she said Nancy Marie sounds too much like what women were called by their slave mistresses. She wanted no part of that! "I love my grandmother," she said, "but I don't want to be called Nancy."

She was a beautiful little girl, very personable and smart. She interacted well with family members and classmates and was a delight to be around. She changed her name to Sakeenah (peaceful, tranquil) and asked that we, the family, not call her Nancy Marie. By the time she was sixteen years old, she'd legally changed her name to Sakeenah Sabree.

While yet a little girl, an incident happened between Sakeenah (Nancy) and Grandpa Obadiah (Mama's father). He was holding baby Nancy in his lap and had rubbed his rugged whiskers against her cheek. Before we realized what was going on, Baby Nancy hauled off and slapped Grandpa Obie on his face, and climbed out of his lap! He laughed so hard because he couldn't believe it. Baby Nancy was usually very mild-mannered. She fooled us all that time. Grandpa Obadiah chuckled and said," Nasty Nan don't you be so mean"! All we could do was laugh.

One of the most challenging experiences of my life occurred in 1957. It was losing the youngest child in the family. Mama had named her Queen Zenobia. Queen was a beautiful and delightful yet determined little girl. She was also very creative and could be very cunning as well. When the spirit hit her, she would try to manipulate Mama to come around to her way of thinking.

Mama was baking a cake, and Queen wanted to lick the bowl. Mama had given her some batter on a spoon and explained that she would be reusing the bowl to make another cake. Queenie could only see it her way and was determined to lick and did not want to wait. So, she gave Mama a piece of her mind, "Why are you so mean and hateful?" We all laughed when we heard her say that to Mama. We knew Queenie was sincere; that was the way she felt about it.

She was very astute for a two-year-old, showing this especially when she heard everyone preparing for Dad's arrival from work. Queenie was the youngest and the center of attention. After Dad cleaned the cement dust off, he would ask, "Where is Queenie?" He would pick Queenie up and throw her into the air.

Dad would question Queenie about her habit of taking off her clothes in the middle of the day, especially her panties. I think she would have wet them and did not like the feel of wet panties on her bottom. The other problem was that Queenie was constantly losing her shoes. Most of the time, she did not wear shoes. Each day when she'd hear us say it was time for dad to come home, Queen would make a hasty run to try and find her shoes and put on some clean panties before dad came into the house. After he'd greeted everybody in the kitchen and kissed Mama, his routine was to ask where his baby was. That was Queenie's cue to come. She would make her grand entrance and jump into Dad's arms.

One night Mama had been searching through the book, *Back to Eden*. It was one of her favorite reference books for treating ailments. It was filled with natural herbal remedies. Whenever we had family members not feeling well, we knew Mama would find the solution. We had been complaining of stomach aches. Mama gave each of us a tablespoon of Oil of Wintergreen along with a little sugar to alleviate the tummy aches. It seemed that Queenie really liked the concoction and climbed to the area where she thought it might be. When Queenie climbed up to the cabinet where Mama stored the Wintergreen, Mama discovered the next day, that she had consumed quite a bit of it.

Queenie and I shared the hide-a-way bed in the living room. I was awakened by Queenie moaning and groaning. Her forehead was warm to the touch. I took Queenie's temperature and told Mama and Dad immediately that Queenie had a fever. She was not feeling well at all. Mama gave her a baby aspirin, but she was still feverish. She was not doing any better. Mama and Dad decoded to wait until early morning to take Queenie to the emergency room. I felt very skeptical about waiting; I put cold water on a towel and kept wiping her with it.

Black people understood during this time that the hospital staff was very racist. Black patients in the Inkster-Romulus, Garden City, and Dearborn communities all had to vie for attention at the same hospital. It didn't matter what the emergency was. When Mama and Dad got Queenie to Wayne County General Hospital, she was hot to the touch. They made it known to the admitting clerk several times that Queenie needed immediate attention.

By the time doctors and nurses examined Queenie, it was too late. They attempted to pump her stomach of the poisoning that was in her system (the Oil of Wintergreen had set up poison in her system because of the amount she'd taken). Mama and Dad had sat waiting to be seen for two long hours!

My heart dropped when Mama and Dad came home without Queenie. I cried for days and days. I took the whole thing very hard. I couldn't believe we'd lost my baby sister and she would not be coming back home. I felt sick all over. I grieved for weeks. During this time, I pleaded with G-d to return Queenie to the family and take me in her place. I blamed myself for what had happened. I tuned everything out around me. I became more and more reclusive and more and more withdrawn from family, friends, and everything around me. It was a difficult time for me. I look back now and realize I needed counseling. Of course, there was very little of that available. Most black families didn't have the time nor the resources for counseling.

Of course, Mama and Dad tried to reach out to me and help me understand I certainly was not at fault and that we all had done the best we could. It was just her time, and she had gone to be with Almighty G-d. Many pioneer sisters reached out to me. They wanted to help me understand that Queenie had gone ahead to make way for Mama and Dad, that she would be standing at the gates to provide a way for them when they made their transition. The believers helped in many ways. They prayed and offered condolences to the family. Many brought food and money, and some would sit and talk to give support. Minister Lemuel Hasan advised Mama and Dad about funeral arrangements. The temple secretary coordinated the receipt of donations to the temple to assist Mama and Dad.

I dealt with my grief by reading more: *Little Women, Peter Pan, Swiss Family Robinson, Charlotte's Web* and more. I listened to Mama's music collection: The Platters, Nat King Cole, Johnny

Mathis, and others. And of course, Mama kept me busy with cooking, cleaning, and washing. This helped. Knowing that Mama depended on me to help her was consoling.

Mama started going to night school to learn bookkeeping and accounting so she could help Dad with his construction company. By doing this, she could handle the bookkeeping required for the business. Now that Dad was beginning to pick up more business, there would be three to five employees all the time. The employees were Muslim brothers, relatives, and neighbors. Taxes had to be deducted. While she was preparing herself for the task, my parents were able to find a Muslim, Brother Everett, a certified public accountant, to do taxes and other necessary paperwork.

Even though we lost one child, there were still six children in the family, and in 1958 my mother was expecting twins. She had some of the strangest cravings. We knew that when she was expecting, she would sometimes crave Argo starch, but Mama took things a step further. She wanted sour dirt, and she would have my grandfather in Alabama send it to her through the mail. Something else she craved was Fleischmann's yeast cakes. She was already blowing up so quickly that we were afraid the yeast was making her belly expand even more! Mama was so big with the twins that when she'd lie down, all we could see was her belly. We would have to come close to see her face. Praise Be to G-d; the twins were born healthy, and they were big babies for twins. Mama and Dad named them Benita and Bernard; they had a combined weight of 13 ½ pounds. They were born August 18th, 1959.

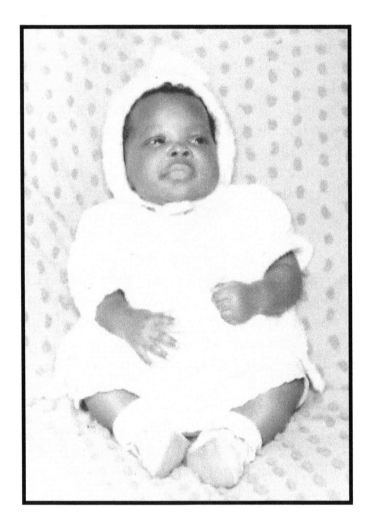

Baby Queen Zenobia

CHAPTER SIX

MGT, GCC, AND ME

1963 was a memorable year. In August there was the March on Washington, a gathering of about 250,000 civil rights demonstrators on the National Mall. A highlight of the event was the famous *I Have a Dream* speech delivered by Reverend Dr. Martin Luther King, Jr. at the Lincoln Memorial.

Later the same year, in November, President John F. Kennedy was assassinated as his presidential motorcade passed through Dealey Plaza in Dallas, Texas. This took place in full view of thousands watching the procession in person and on national television. Two days later, television viewers saw the alleged assassin, Lee Harvey Oswald, shot and killed by a bar owner, Jack Ruby. Of great significance for Nation of Islam Muslims was the untimely public statement that Malcolm X made in New York concerning the assassination. He said of it that "the chickens have come home to roost... chickens coming home to roost never made me sad, always made me glad." The response of Honorable Elijah Muhammad to Malcolm's statement was to publicly censor him and to relieve him of speaking privileges for a time. All of this snowballed into a breach developing between Honorable Elijah Muhammad and Minister Malcolm. What ensued is well known sad history.

Earlier the same year, in June, I graduated from Inkster High School. By the time of graduation, I had adapted to the public-school environment, and that environment had adapted to me. I wore my NOI Muslim attire (no head covering), no problem. I was Sister Lynice X who belonged to an organization that did not subscribe to turning the other cheek to the white man. I dressed differently and I ate different food, which I shared with classmates. Many school-mates wanted to know what I had to say about the civil rights move-ment. During my three years at Inkster High many of my school-mates accepted Islam. I had followed the advice of my parents who encouraged me to be comfortable with myself and exemplify the teachings I followed by how I carried myself. I did this through par-ticipation in various school activities, among them the Debate Club, the Future Teachers Club, and the Yearbook Club.

In addition to attending school regularly, I babysat and ironed clothes for neighbors to make extra money. And I worked for Ms. Castle, a neighbor who lived a few blocks away. I helped her with clothes she took in from white people. Ms. Castle was an elementary teacher who dressed the part of a schoolmarm, with her hair neatly pulled back in a bun. She wore a blueish pink and grey house dress that probably had been washed over 100 times, to the point of los-ing its luster. Her home was reflective of who she was. It was neatly arranged, with a couch, a chair, a picture representing Jesus, and a couple of photographs, and plants. There were only necessary fur-nishings in the house, including a bookcase and a sewing machine. Ms. Castle wore lace-up black oxford shoes.

She interviewed me concerning my ironing skill. She gave me a shirt to demonstrate my ironing technique. As I ironed, she explained that I should pay special attention to the shirt's collar and sleeves, making sure no "cat faces" (wrinkles) were left.

My brothers James and Jonathan had paper routes. They took pride in distributing papers and having satisfied customers. The customers would make sure they were paid, often giving them tips and wonderful holiday gifts. Dad set an excellent example for my brothers to follow with his work ethic. In addition to their paper route and their wrestling and self-defense classes, my brothers would work with dad doing construction work on occasion. My brother James said that doing the construction work made him determined to complete a college education. He was grateful for the opportunity but did not want to do the hard work for the rest of his life.

My parents encouraged me to do two things in particular after graduation. Mama wanted me to get my driver's license. Dad wanted me to attend business school for a secretarial program so I could earn a living and be able to support myself. I had no interest in getting a driver's license at that time. I felt that people drove too recklessly and did not want to encounter these drivers. But when I learned it would only take about six weeks to get my driver's license, I enrolled in the driver training course.

My parents expressed their concern that many young girls are in a hurry to get married after high school; they forget about getting an education. I assured them they did not have to worry about me in that respect. Nevertheless, they both encouraged me with all the intensity they could muster. They wanted all their children to complete a high school education, and a college education if that was what they wanted. They wanted us to have skills or training in a trade for earning a decent living.

My parents expressed how proud they were of me, their first-born, for having completed High School. It was a big accomplishment. Still, they said, it was only the beginning, and my dad encouraged me to think about going to a business college to take typing and shorthand. They suggested that taking a business course would be very beneficial to my future, that I should consider this course of action so I would have something to fall back on and be able to support myself. They were not discouraging me from becoming a teacher, but I needed to be concerned about taking care of myself. My father reminded me that there were quite a few children under me he would have to help.

In keeping with the advice of my parents, I earned certificates for shorthand and for typing. I took courses at Henry Ford Community College, some to enhance my secretarial skills and others to prepare me to pursue a degree in elementary education. When I attempted to become a degree candidate, I learned I lacked prerequisites in English, mathematics, and biology. I would have to pay to take the needed courses. I enrolled, but after a few months I resolved that it was better for me to work and save money. So, I set out to find a job.

I was seventeen. Searching for a job was very challenging. I was rescued by President of the United States, Lyndon Baines Johnson. He had declared a "war on poverty." This led to the to the "landmark" federal legislation of 1964, the Economic Opportunity Act. In Inkster that act took the form of an operation called Total Action Against Poverty, or TAAP. The agency referred me to a company housed in the top floors of a 12-story warehouse. I took a position with R.L. Polk as a production typist. I was one of about 30 people who competed in the production of address labels. Consistent losers in the competition would soon get a pink slip. I was hoping for one, but no such luck because of my training in high school; I had a typing speed around 60 wpm. The job was not a pleasant experience. I clocked in at 10 p. m. and clocked out at 7 a. m. There never was enough time to do things I needed to do, get sufficient sleep, and then get to work on time. Not counting babysitting, this was my first job. I made five dollars and hour. I was very grateful for the money, but there had to be a better way.

TAAP came to my rescue. A counselor directed me to an opening with the Detroit News. They were hiring copy clerks and reference clerks. I was hired as a copy clerk. The Detroit News job was more to my liking. The schedule was more realistic for me.

I had thought about being a writer along with being a teacher. Somehow, I was convinced that if I prepared myself as a teacher, I could work my way back to writing if I wanted to. Of course, there was no writing required of me. I was grateful to be in an atmosphere with professional writers. There were 12 to 15 professional writers. There was one black editor and one black secretary, and me. I reflected on the situation, and I felt that we were the tokens needed at this time. I talked with several writers about their work schedules and about the preparation required to become a copywriter. I worked in this position for a year before being promoted to reference clerk.

In balancing work and remaining active in the temple, we would strive to keep our religious beliefs a priority. Our family would attend temple meetings regularly on Sundays. We had to be there promptly at 2:00 or a little before. If we were running late for any reason, we had to call and let the officials know that we would be late and give a reasonable explanation as to why we were late. We were required to let them know what time we would be there. This was a part of the discipline practiced by the Nation of Islam.

Each time we attended a meeting at the temple, whether it was a general temple meeting, MGT, and GCC (Muslim Girls Training and General Civilization Classes) meetings, or a special meeting, everyone had to be searched. It did not matter who you were; it was a required procedure everyone had to undergo. You would be searched from head to toe. If you had something that was not allowed in the meeting, it would be checked and returned upon leaving. Some of the things not allowed in temple meetings: metal nail files, pocketknives, guns, anything that might do bodily harm to someone.

At MGT meetings, we were separated according to our age and, according to how long you had been an active member of the community. You were also grouped according to how advanced you were in knowing the lessons that had been given to you and how frequently you attended the classes. In the classes, we were taught how to prepare to be good Muslim wives and mothers, how to cook healthy meals, sew, and dress modestly. We learned to respect our husbands and all brothers.

It was gratifying to be matched with a pioneer sister like Sister Marie Joshua, Sister Bernestine Muhammad, Sister Nettie Mae, Sister Henrietta, and many others. The pioneer sisters lovingly shared all they knew with us. One of the lessons that we learned on an MGT night was how to prepare whole wheat cinnamon rolls. Sister Joshua was the one in the kitchen; she was one of my favorite cooks at the temple. Mother Joshua shared with the sisters in her group how to make cinnamon rolls. Using the dough left from the whole wheat bread, divided into different sections, rolled into circles about 1 1/2 inch in diameter. We would then combine the softened butter mixture consisting of cinnamon sugar and vanilla over the dough and roll carefully so that you do not lose the filling. You then cut and place the rolls in the pan. Then just wait for the rising to complete. The aroma was delightful. The taste was even better, especially after we drizzled the icing on top. Yum-yum, this was the beginning of being inspired to bake, in addition to being in the kitchen with my mother on 4151 Henry Street. MGT & GCC training classes were held on Thursday evenings. (The special training for the males was the Fruit of Islam classes that were held on Monday evening.)

One fun thing was practicing and executing drills, which demanded a lot of practice. Drilling required alertness and quick thinking. One great benefit of the drill team was that it allowed the young Muslim women to demonstrate their skills and creativity to the seniors. Following the cadence, we moved quickly and precisely. Meanwhile, my mother and other sisters would be learning new techniques for cooking and preparing foods. Pioneer sisters shared that Master Fard Muhammad told them to learn to can and preserve food. He told them there would come a time when we would be unable to go to stores to buy food. When food was plentiful, they should buy up fresh vegetables and fruits. They should learn to use a pressure cooker and canning jars, and to teach each other how to can, making sure that content and date labeling was accurate. Sisters worked on canning in class at the temple, and they perfected their learning by visiting each other's homes to assist each other.

Nation of Islam life was not always as sweet as cinnamon rolls. The goal of Honorable Elijah Muhammad was to root out of his followers (and Black Americans generally) the Negro, the Colored, and Worse. But we were a work in progress. Sometimes because of our "baggage" we made life less than sweet for our brothers and sisters.

My father was an example of what Honorable Elijah Muhammad wanted for us. Dad was a man of outstanding character. His word was his bond, an important precept in the Nation. He would say he was raised in a family that was not the best because his father was absent and that because of this he was motivated to become a responsible family man and a man of integrity. But I think about him, and what comes to mind is that being raised in such a family in Alabama was not the same as being raised the same way in a big city like Detroit. That kind of upbringing in Detroit was less likely to motivate a young positively man and more likely to do him long term damage.

There were brothers at the temple for whom the rooting out of Negro-Colored-Worse was taking longer than it was taking for others. I recall brothers skipping out on the responsibility of seeing that sisters had rides home after meetings. This was policy that came down from Honorable Elijah Muhammad. There were times when Dad made three or more trips from the temple to transport sisters before bringing us home to Inkster while brothers who had cars and lived in Detroit were nowhere to be found.

It might have been these same brothers who found themselves facing utility shut-offs for not having paid their bills. They would come to Dad for help. Of course, he would help them. He was pledged to help his black brother in difficulty. His word was his bond. Mama would help too. She often got on the phone with the utility company to work out extensions and payment arrangements for those borrowing money. Yes, we were a work in progress.

And progress was slow for some sisters too. It was Nation of Islam policy that women not wear makeup. Dad used to say that all his daughters were beautiful and that we should not hide that beauty with makeup. So, makeup was not an issue for me. However, it did become an issue one day when I was seventeen or so.

I visited the office of the temple secretary for some reason. A sister lieutenant or squad leader was present. She claimed I was wearing makeup. Had this claim become an official charge I was looking at Class C restriction, thirty days of ostracism. She called someone to come to the office to verify her claim. In a sense, I was under arrest, a lot like a traffic stop. Because of my personal standards, I was embarrassed and humiliated. Eventually it was determined that I was not wearing makeup. I received an apology and was "released."

I was hurt. I told my parents. They agreed I had been the victim of envy—or some other emotion stirred up by Satan. Yes, we were a work in progress. Overall, progress makes life sweet, but that does not happen overnight.

CHAPTER SEVEN

JACKSON, MISSISSIPPI

A t the time of this writing, Masjid Muhammad in Jackson, Mississippi, is on track to relocate to a new building on nine acres. With respect to size and aspirations, the congregation has outgrown what has been its residence since 1999. The envisioned Masjid Muhammad will be a new construction, one conceptualized by the current congregation and to be financed through its efforts. May G-d make it so.

If you are reading this at a time when plans have not come to fruition, you are invited to help move things forward with a contribution to the masjid at its current location: Masjid Muhammad; 6100 Floral Drive; Jackson, MS 39206. You will be honoring the aspirations and hard work that gave rise to Temple No. 78 in 1974, out of which grew Masjid Muhammad after the passing of Honorable Elijah Muhammad. That work was begun in the nineteen sixties by a handful of pioneers led by a young minister named Thomas Shabazz. I had a hand in that hard work of the sixties.

Thomas Young, the son of Jessie James Young and Nettie Young, was not a criminal. But he spent two years in Milan (Michigan) Federal Penitentiary from 1965 to 1967. In fact, he was a model citizen. Having been born in Montrose, Arkansas, he graduated from Vashon High School in St. Louis, Missouri. At Vashon he was an athlete participating in three sports. After Vashon, for two semesters, he attended what is now Harris-Stowe State University in St. Louis. Yes, Thomas was a model citizen, and he was intelligent and strong-willed. His crime was refusing to serve in the military. This was at the height of the Viet Nam War.

Thomas was arrested in Jackson, Mississippi. He had left Harris-Stowe and moved to Detroit, possibly following his brother Alonzo who was already established there. In Detroit, against the objections of Alonzo and most members of his family, Thomas joined the Nation of Islam at Temple No. 1. The minister at Temple No. 1 recognized his talent and referred him to Honorable Elijah Muhammad for ministerial study. He was accepted. Upon completing his studies in Chicago, he was tasked with the responsibility of building a community in Jackson, Mississippi—from scratch.

Thomas went to Jackson and started recruiting. Recruiting was not easy. In many northern cities you could find Nation of Islam teachers soapboxing. This was not possible in southern states. Such behavior on the part of anyone was frowned upon. It went against so-called southern gentility. You would not find white Christians soapboxing. Thomas had been apprised of this in his preparation.

Thomas enjoyed teaching, and he was an eloquent speaker who knew how to deliver the message of Honorable Elijah Muhammad. A street corner discussion with one person could easily have attracted a large audience. That would have been a violation of the protocol. Moreover, he would have been subject to arrest or worse. His mission would be undermined.

Whenever Thomas did pique the interest of someone on the street, he hastened to move the discussion indoors, possibly to a later time, possibly to a place recommended by the listener. In that instance he would encourage the listener to invite others to hear him. Thomas might invite to the meeting others whose interest he had piqued. Eventually some attended the meetings regularly. Some meetings happened on the campus of Jackson State College (the HBCU which is now Jackson State University). In 1965, Thomas was arrested by the FBI for avoiding military service. Those meetings on the campus of Jackson State College may have brought Thomas to the attention of local authorities. So, the mission of Minister Thomas Shabazz was undermined temporarily.

In 1966 I was nineteen. I knew nothing about Jackson, Mississippi, or the activities of Minister Thomas Shabazz. And even though he had come into the Nation at Temple No. 1, neither my parents nor my siblings knew him or about him.

In 1966 I had a bright red 1965 Corvair convertible. I was a reference clerk at the Detroit News. I was doing well in courses at Henry Ford Community College. I was attending meetings and classes at Temple No. 1. Life was good, Praise be to G-d. But 'good' was not good enough. Thoughts of marriage had entered my mind. I floated the idea to Mama. She advised me to pray about it. I did.

Thomas was paroled in the vicinity of Washtenew, Michigan, in 1967. He started attending Washtenaw Junior College. There he met James, my brother, also a student at the college. James brought him to our home to meet the family.

Thomas was intelligent and articulate. He was also a minister. My parents and siblings were impressed. I was curious. I pressed James for more information about him. In the meantime, Thomas sought the permission of my father to discuss with me the possibility of marriage. Permission was granted.

For six months, two or three times a week, Thomas drove thirty miles to Inkster to visit me and my family. We would sit alone and talk, but we were never really alone. Even if no adults were in the house, there were always little curious ears tuned in to wherever Thomas and I happened to be sitting and talking. And of course, sit and talk is all we did.

At the end of that six months the talk turned to a proposal for marriage. Of course, I was not surprised. However, the proposal was shocking in the sense that it shocked me into reality. Some of that reality was a bit disturbing. For me to be Thomas's wife I would have to leave Inkster. Moreover, I would have to move to Jackson, Mississippi. That was not an exciting prospect for a northern black girl. The news from Mississippi regarding black people was not good.

Mississippi was one of the states comprising what was/is known as the "deep south." To black people the clear reference of "deep" is the implacable entrenchment of Jim Crow values. "N_g_h, don't let the sun set on your black [behind] in this town." Alabama, where I was born, is also a "deep south" state, but I had left Alabama at age three. The marriage proposal was to a northern black girl.

Jackson is the capital of Mississippi. It was also home to a branch of the White Citizens Council, a group formed in Mississippi in 1954 to resist school desegregation and oppose all civil rights activism. In 1963 a member of this organization assassinated NAACP president Medgar Evers in his driveway in Jackson. (The assassin, Byron De La Beckwith, was not convicted of the murder until 1994, having been acquitted initially.) In February 1967 a car bomb killed Wharlston Jackson, the thirty-six-year-old treasurer of the Natchez, Mississippi, NAACP. Natchez is a hundred miles from Jackson.

Honorable Elijah Muhammad explicitly directed his followers away from civil rights activism. In fact, in a sense, the Nation was opposed to the civil rights movement. Of course, the White Citizens Council, Ku Klux Klan, and white people generally did not know this. Thomas was on a dangerous mission. He would be perceived as leading a black activist organization, one growing in strength nationwide. He was also introducing a new religion to the south, one—as misunderstood by most—that preached hatred of white people and that rejected Jesus.

Thomas saw himself being responsible for protecting the small Muslim community that was growing under him. He was asking me to help him with his mission, to help him stay strong. I didn't know. I had to think about that.

There was another issue that caused me pause. Maybe it wasn't as large in my mind as the first issue, but it was real. When Thomas proposed I was nineteen. He was twenty-eight, nine years older than me. He was a grown man. I was a girl. That's how I saw it. I discussed this with girlfriends. Some said I was being silly and that I should be happy to have a proposal from mature and serious man. The Muslim girls were especially impressed by his being a minister. Still, I didn't know. I made Thomas wait. He returned to Jackson. We communicated for three months before I accepted his proposal.

We set the wedding date for September 10th, 1967. It was in June that I accepted his proposal. I had less than three months to prepare. One of the things I did was to make myself debt free by arranging with James to assume ownership of my car once I left Inkster.

As for the wedding, I made all the arrangements. Mama wanted to help more than she did, but she was pregnant with number eleven, my youngest sibling, my sister Iatrice. A Christian minister, Reverend Grant, officiated because there was no one among the local Muslims who could legally officiate. The ceremony and reception were held in the LeMoyne Gardens Community Center in Inkster.

My friends did a masterful job with decorating the center. Close to a hundred attended. Mama Nettie, Thomas's mother, was there. My mother was stunning in her hot pink dress, the same hot pink as the dresses of my bridesmaids. I wore a beautiful white gown. Dad gave me away. The food was delicious, especially the very expensive three-tiered cake. It was a wonderful event, a happy event. Mama cried.

We spent our wedding night at the La Quinta in downtown Detroit. Our honeymoon began the next day, with the nearly one-thousand-mile drive from Detroit to Jackson. We stopped and spent a short time in St. Louis, Missouri, where I met Thomas's father and siblings. It was an exciting time.

The honeymoon ended, you might say, as soon as we arrived in Jackson. Our residence was a furnished apartment near the campus of Jackson State College that Thomas had rented right before coming back to Michigan for the wedding. He had not lived in it. In fact, when we arrived the previous tenant was just finalizing her departure. The apartment was dirty, and we had to clean it. That is, I had to clean it. Thomas immediately dove into his job as minister. Cleaning took me three days.

Thomas introduced me to the Muslim community within a week of our arrival. The core comprised about ten young people, men and women. Intelligent, pleasant, and well mannered; they were very excited about being Muslims and about the challenges lying ahead of them. I spent memorable times with the sisters, especially in my first two years. I shared what I had learned at Temple No. 1, the wisdom I had garnered from Muslim Girls Training and General Civilization Class. We discussed *How to Eat to Live* and *Message to the Black Man*, the books by Honorable Elijah Muhammad. I shared what I had learned from Mama about baking, especially wheat bread and bean pies.

The little community, sisters and brothers, was a special group of people. They were southern black people. They didn't have the sharp edge that blacks tend to take on when they become northerners. These people were gentle. And they were courageous.

Being "black Muslims," they were bucking a lot of norms. Of course, there were the racist whites. But they also had to answer to, and possibly disappoint, their own Christian, and largely religious, family members and friends. And they may even have had to explain their positions to activists in the civil rights movement; to SNCC members, to those "sitting in" in nearby Tougaloo, and to those who had marched in the large 1966 march in Jackson commemorating the 1963 murder of Medgar Evans.

This is reasonable speculation. I don't recall any discussions along these lines. What I vividly recall is their kindness. I recall attempting to can tomatoes because Thomas thought it a necessity, totally ignoring that I was six months pregnant. I fell asleep and was awakened by exploding canning jars and tomatoes splattered everywhere. I had done something wrong and wasn't awake to catch my mistake. In a panic, I called Sister Laura for advice. She and her husband Brother Joe came right over and managed the disaster.

Building a Nation of Islam community required a lot of work. I recall the names of some of the people either Thomas or I could always rely upon for help: Sister Barbara, Sister Cynthia, Sister Delphine, Sister Henrene, Sister Laura (mentioned above), Brother Charles, Brother Jessie, Brother Joe (mentioned above).

There was one Muslim who did much to make my stay in Jackson comfortable. Jo Mary Smith. She was not a Muslim. She was a Christian, a very good Christian. Her beautiful spirit matched that of the beautiful sisters who made up our little community.

Ms. Smith was a widow with fifteen children. She and Thomas had met some time before my arrival, and she was very impressed with the work he was doing. When I arrived, she adopted us into her family. We had Sunday dinner in her home often. When we got the first invitation, Thomas explained to Ms. Smith that we could not eat out of the same pots and pans in which she prepared ham and pigs feet. By the next week, she had purchased a new set of pots and pans, instructing her children that they were only to be used when preparing meals for Thomas and Lynice. By 3 p. m. on those Sundays, Ms. Smith and her daughters had prepared two complete meals. Those for Thomas and me often consisted of baked chicken, potato salad, green beans, iced tea, and peach cobbler.

Soon after arriving in Jackson, I registered for classes at Utica Community College. It happened that Ms. Smith's youngest daughter, Juanita, was a student at the college. That was a great blessing. We would meet and take the bus to the school together. I completed the fall semester, but that was it. I was pregnant with Aleisha. She was born July 7th, 1968. Mama came when it was time for me to deliver. Iatrice was with her. Iatrice had been born just five months earlier.

Even with Iatrice in tow, Mama was a tremendous help. She shopped and cleaned. She became friends with my neighbors, including Ms. Jo Mary Smith. I am certain she made a profound impression on those neighbors. They were black, and they were Christians. They had been very welcoming to me and Thomas, but I am sure they had their concerns. Of course, Mama knew this. She had been there. I doubt that Mama did much explaining about the Nation. Instead, she surprised them with her knowledge of the Bible. And she won them over with her vibrant spirit. I am certain no better ambassador for al-Islam had ever set foot in the state of Mississippi. Mama visited several times, helped, and did her quiet dawah work.

In the spring of 1969, Aleisha and I went to Inkster and stayed for six weeks. I was pregnant. Our family was growing, but my marriage was not. It was failing. I was in distress. My home was not the happy home I had left in Inkster. Throughout my life I had seen Dad work long hard hours, longer and harder than those worked by Thomas. But I never got the sense that Mama felt neglected or that she felt overburdened by having to care for a house full of children while helping Dad with his business. The sense I had gotten was that Mama felt she was Dad's partner, one Dad depended on and consulted. When Mama visited me—bringing her eleventh child—I was amazed at her lively spirit and tireless energy. In contrast, when I visited her, I was tired and listless. I was coming from a home where I felt neglected and where I was never consulted about Muslim community matters, family matters, or my own needs.

Thomas was focused exclusively on what he had been sent by Honorable Elijah Muhammad to do. The little community bought a duplex. Thomas had knowledge of building construction because that is how he a made a living. He and the brothers broke down walls and did the other things required to transform the duplex into one building, 1208 Jones Street, the building that was designated Temple No. 78 in 1974.

Maybe Thomas had other concerns. Now I am certain he did, but he never spoke to me about them. The FBI must have been a concern. He had been on their radar screen since 1965 when he was arrested and imprisoned. FBI agents once visited and questioned me. The topic was Thomas. I don't recall their questions. I do recall not being able to answer any of them. At that time, I was very much a homebody, and I honestly had no answers. Even if I did, I would not have given any answers. I had been raised in the Nation of Islam, and the FBI was who they were. Shonuff.

I look back through the lens of updated history and realize the visit was significant. This was the FBI of J. Edgar Hoover, who had resolved to protect America from the danger of black activism. We now look back and understand the death of Malcolm in light of this resolve. And the death of Dr. King. And the death of Fred Hampton. And others.

Thomas could very well have been on a list of potential hits. But the investigators probably determined that, while his profile suggested dangerous potential, Thomas was not a threat. For one, he and his community were not involved in sit-ins and SNCC activity in nearby Tougaloo. The focus of these Muslims was not on politics but on establishing their religion. That religion, perceived as anti-white and anti-Jesus, was troublesome, but it was not an existential threat.

In fact, one aspect of the anti-white part was particularly appealing to the White Citizens Council. The Nation of Islam excluded whites from membership and denounced interracial marriage. Of course, these positions of Honorable Elijah Muhammad represented political strategy and not racism on his part. But the White Citizens Council did not know this. So, the FBI was satisfied with our politics, and the White Citizens Council was okay with our religion.

Talib, my second child, was born October 7th, 1970. The pregnancy went full term, but Talib did not make it. His lungs were not strong. He required a respirator. He passed from this life forty-eight hours after his birth. I was traumatized. Thomas suggested that Talib had gone ahead to prepare a way for his parents and sibling. I found some consolation in this. We both found consolation in the birth of our third child, our son, Yusuf. He arrived October 4th, 1971.

Khalilah Ali, the wife of Muhammad Ali, had an uncle, Calvin, who lived in Meridian, about ninety minutes from Jackson. He was among a few brothers who often came to our meetings. Whenever Khalilah visited him, he would bring her and her children to a meeting. Of course, as wife of the minister I would assume the role of official hostess. We would always sit and chat, discussing children and related matters. We exchanged numbers, promising to keep in touch, but that never happened because of how my life evolved.

It was probably one of these visits that prompted community sisters to do something that caused me embarrassment and stirred emotions beyond that. There was attractive Sister Khalilah Ali, wife of Muhammad Ali, dressed modestly and beautifully. She was sitting alongside attractive Sister Lynice Shabazz, wife of Minister Thomas Shabazz, dressed modestly—but less than beautifully—quite a bit less. The sisters chipped in, bought fabric, and one of them made me a beautiful dress.

I accepted the gift graciously, but I was embarrassed. They didn't mind the embarrassment, assuming it was feigned. No, the embarrassment was real. Those wonderful sisters didn't realize that what they had done was something Thomas never would have thought to do.

Thomas was insensitive, neglectful, and sometimes inconsiderate concerning my needs. When I complained, he responded that I was rebellious. I look back and realize his attitude was due to his lack of maturity regarding women. And it was a function of the pressures he was under, pressures related to his community responsibilities, pressures about which I had no knowledge. I realize this now, but then, in my early twenties, with two children and having lost a child, I was depressed. I was miserable.

Thomas bought us a house. He informed me about the house a day or so before the designated moving day! That was the last straw. I was livid and was not consoled by his informing me that the community had helped him with the purchase. I refused to help with the moving, leaving that to Thomas and the brothers.

I lived in our new home for less than a year. It was clear to Thomas that I was miserable. He suggested I return to Inkster. Toward the end of the year, I did. Eventually Thomas and I divorced.

CHAPTER EIGHT

HARD TRIALS AND SEPARATION

I was Leaving Jackson, Mississippi. It is 1972. I am now twenty-five years old and have spent five years of my life striving to be the best wife, helpmate, and mother I could be. I have so many questions in my mind about how and why this has occurred. Why would Thomas Shabazz send his family back to Detroit at this time? These are all questions that I have asked myself, but only time will reveal the answer. I struggle to determine what if anything I did wrong. I'm trying to keep pride and dignity. I'm married to a Muslim minister, who was taught to respect and hold the women in high regard, his wife, his mother, and all black women.

I felt the brother I was married to would do the right thing. I had given him the benefit of the doubt. I was disappointed. I felt Thomas would take on the obligations put before him even though we were not together. I learned this was wishful thinking.

My mother, being the wise woman she was, tried to console me. At the same time, she tried to help me to see the reality of the situation. The reality was that I must go to the people I call the "devil" and get help for me and my children. I knew that if she and Dad were able to, they would help me and the children with no questions asked. However, they were still raising four children. Besides, it was not my parents' responsibility. The responsibility was Thomas's and mine! I knew I would have to go to the Department of Children and Family Services because there were no other alternatives.

Thomas had sent one hundred dollars during the three months I resided with my parents. The money was not enough to cover the cost of my groceries. I called Jackson but received no response. Eventually, I received a long letter from Thomas in which he tells me he no longer wants anything to do with me. He doesn't mention the children but says "You are on your own." He writes, "What about the FOI?" He tells me I must stop depending on him and make myself available to the FOI.

I Could not believe this! The way this man had insisted that I completely depend upon him while we were together. I am without any resources, but even more disheartening was another part of the story I'm hearing. Thomas has married one of the sisters in Mississippi who has five children. Of course, it couldn't be legal; we are still legally married according to Michigan's law. His story was that she needed a husband more than I did. I had a family and only two children. (His children!) I wanted to scream.

Mama had to shake me from my depression, she and a pioneer sister, Mother Mary Pasha. She was related to our family by marriage. Mother Mary's son Carl Pasha had married one of my mother's younger sisters, Dorothy Ma. (She has since changed her name to Bayyinah Pasha.) Mother Mary put it to me quite bluntly. "Lynice, you are not the first woman to be separated from her husband, and you won't be the last. What's most important for you now is realizing that you have two children dependent upon you. If you don't feed them, they don't eat. If you don't put a roof over their head, they will not have a place to stay. Stop feeling sorry for yourself. Have some backbone and some grit."

I loved Mother Mary's spirit. She would not allow me to have a pity party. It was the shock treatment I needed to bring me back to reality. "Know that Allah will help you if you make an effort." I must swallow my pride and go to the Department of Family and Children Services and seek help for my emergency needs. I was thankful to Almighty G-d for taking the blinders off. I'm so grateful to Mother Mary, who made me face reality and did not sugar coat it. I am grateful to my family, brothers, sisters, mother, and father for allowing the time that I needed for coming to a better understanding.

I made an appointment to see the minister at that time, Minister Hasty Muhammad. He listened attentively. He sympathized and empathized. He told me not to let feelings of depression get the best of me. Patience and perseverance are the key. "Allah will make way for you and your children. Sister, the mosque is unable to give you any financial support at this time."

I gradually began to pull myself out of the mud. Making prayers, reading inspirational books, talking to people who had experienced similar difficulties. One such person was Trevia Miles, who had only recently become a member of NOI. (Her brother and sister-in-law, Carey and Paulette, with whom I was very familiar, were already members. I had gone to school with some of her family members.) Word of mouth carries. She heard I was looking for a place to stay, and she responded that she was looking to share the house and its expenses with someone. It was a three-bedroom house that she was renting. There was more space than she needed. It was a perfect match for my two children and me. I could give Mom and Dad and the family some breathing room. Thank Allah for His Mercy!

In 1972, my daughter Aleisha was five and Yusuf was two. In my mind they were the main reason for my existence during this period. This helped push me forward. I recall Mama saying that if you take one step to help yourself, Allah will take two towards you. I can truly attest to that. Things did begin to open up for me. My number one concern was to make sure that Aleisha and Yusuf had proper clothing for the Michigan weather, that the two of them stayed healthy. I was blessed because I had Mama and my sisters Renee and Sakinah to assist with the care of the children.

Having Mama at hand was especially comforting. She knew how to keep children healthy. Once, when I visited from Jackson, Yusuf, who was nine months old, had a rash that the doctor was treating with medication. It was the second time for this outbreak. Mama suggested I stop applying the medication and instead use an herbal cure she prepared. It was a mixture of fenugreek and comfrey. She steeped the herbs and made a tea which we gave to Yusuf in a bottle. Mom took the seeds of the fenugreek tea and made a poultice by putting the seeds into a piece of cheesecloth and applied it directly to the rash. She continued this for about ten days. The rash completely healed and did not return.

Mama also suggested I feed Yusuf regular table food, since I was not eating enough to produce milk sufficient to satisfy Yusuf. I was having to nurse him frequently. I started feeding him cream of wheat, oatmeal, bean soup, applesauce, carrots, squash, and other foods that were appropriate for him.

There was something that both children struggled and suffered with. It was bronchial asthma. It was especially consequential during certain times of the year. After playing outside, they would come into the house breathing hard, coughing, sometimes wheezing, and would sometimes develop a rash. Of course, my first instinct was to take them to the doctor, and sometimes a doctor's intervention was necessary. I also learned that if the occurrence was not severe, I could manage it myself by keeping a cool head, helping them relax and breathe, and not feed them foods that would contribute to inflammation, foods such as milk, butter, and cheese. As they grew older, their immune systems became stronger. They were able to outgrow the asthmatic episodes.

When I moved back to Inkster following my separation, I was extremely thin compared to what is usual for me. The reason was the breakup, my depressive moods. I was suffering. I was about one hundred twenty pounds, small for me. My sister Renee has never allowed me to live this down. She still teases me about a particular incident. A high school friend did not recognize me. She looked at me and said I should be sure to tell Lynice hello for me. I tried to let her know that I was Lynice, but she found it difficult to acknowledge the slightest possibility I was who I said I was. My face was thin and solemn, not joyful and full as it usually was. Friends would see me and inquire as to what had happened. Those who knew me well would not let me get away with, "I'm fine." They would press me, and I would assure them that I was fine; however, I'm sure they could read between the lines and realized I was not myself. What kept me going was that I had to continue being strong for my two children. As my mother would say, "They didn't ask to be here."

Thanks to Allah, things began to open up for me. I could begin to concentrate on myself. One of the first things I needed to do was have some Islamic garments made and find someplace to order outfits that were ready prepared. Muhammad Speaks newspaper solved both problems. I was able to order Islamic outfits and see a list of people I could contact to make garments. Because I signed for DFACS benefits, I was eligible for benefits for my children as well as myself. Since I had attended business college, I qualified to work for Head Start. I worked as a secretary and receptionist for thirty hours weekly at minimum wage and continued to receive regular benefits.

Again, I'm grateful for Allah's mercy. The job was a two-fold blessing. I was able to help myself and my family. And the experience was one that gave me a much-needed esteem boost. I interacted professionally with dynamic African Americans, most of them women. While I was hired to be a receptionist and do secretarial work, I was able to step outside that role and render guidance and help to parents of children. I took pride in the fact that staff, administrators, and clients were able to take note that it was a Muslim rendering this help. I worked at this job for two years. Then I began taking classes at Madonna College (now Madonna University).

During my time at Head Start, I met a very wonderful Caucasian girl who was about the same age as me. She reaffirmed my faith in human nature. We talked and shared pleasantries over several months. She was a temporary worker. She was very positive, and we discussed many things. I learned she was of the Jewish faith, and I shared with her about my being a Muslim, and a Nation of Islam believer. I felt very awkward even though I was a mature woman. I had never been this conversant with a Caucasian. However, I liked her and did want to get to know her better. When she asked if she could be my friend, I said something that came out before I could take the time to think about it. "I said, "You can't be my friend because you are a devil by nature." I could see that this statement was a crushing blow, and I was sorry I said it.

She was the bigger person. I became ill with a bad cold. She went so far as to look up my address in the employee records and hand deliver my check to me. Of course, I thanked her and let her know how much I appreciated this gesture. When I think of many things I've done, I realize this was not me, that I was parroting what I thought to be our beliefs. Although I never laid eyes on this person again, I believe with all my heart and soul that she knew that what I said was not what was meant… I was repeating something passed on to me. From this incident, I learned that we must all search our hearts and souls for what is right.

I loved much of what the Nation stood for. There were many things I could not accept. Saying that all white people are devils did not speak to my soul. Saying that Master Fard Muhammad is G-d did not speak to my soul. Saying that the black man is G-d did not speak to my soul. I take pride in knowing that I never tried to teach these tenets to my children. The Qur'an says the best of us are those who have good manners, good character, and are good to others. I taught this to my children, and I taught them to treat others as you would have them treat you. I'm grateful that Allah has guided me to a better understanding.

QURAN 4:19

G-d instructs men to be nice to their wives and to treat them well to the best of their ability: "And live with them in kindness..." (Quran 4:19) The Messenger of G-d said the most perfect of believers in belief are the best of them in character. The best of you are those who are the best to their women.

The noblest in the sight of Allah are the most righteous. Source: Ṣaḥīḥ al-Bukhari 3194, Grade: Muttafaqun Alayhi

CHAPTER NINE

PICKING UP THE PIECES

M ost of the years of the seventies were difficult for me, a period of trial and test. But I look back and see an interesting coincidence. I see my life as a microcosm of what was occurring in the Nation of Islam generally. Those years were years of struggle, a period of trial and test for the Nation.

There was the passing of Mother Clara, the wife of Honorable Elijah Muhammad, in 1972. Then there was the passing of Honorable Elijah Muhammad in 1975. We saw their son, Warith Deen, stand in at major events prior to the passing of his father because his father was experiencing illness and general physical weakness. These were years of uncertainty and even anguish for many believers.

The years following the passing of Honorable Elijah Muhammad were not times of uncertainty and anguish as much as they were times of confusion. Upon the passing of his father, Warith Deen became Supreme Minister of the Nation of Islam. By 1976 the organization had gone through two name changes to become the American Muslim Mission, led by Warith, whose title became Imam Warith Deen Mohammed. Temples became mosques, to be led by imams rather than 'ministers.'

There were other changes. One of the most significant, causing considerable confusion, was the disbanding of the Fruit of Islam (FOI). I never actually spoke with Dad about this change, but I am certain he was unsettled by it. When Louis Farrakhan broke with Imam Mohammed and revived the Nation of Islam under his leadership, he re-instituted FOI, among other traditional NOI features. All my brothers went with Louis Farrakhan.

I have learned that this confusion played out in communities around the country. It played out around me in Inkster as well as in my personal life. Muslims in Inkster, especially the younger ones, had become dissatisfied with the lack of progressiveness of what was now the Detroit mosque, especially concerning Inkster and nearby Romulus. The effort to bring people into Islam was weak, and the effort to teach those already in was just as weak. It was decided that a mosque was necessary in Inkster.

There was a brother in Inkster who had been a minister in a southern city. Maybe he was the one who initiated the discussion about having our own mosque. I am not certain. We reached out to him. He was the natural choice for leading us. He was a fiery and articulate teacher of the doctrines of Honorable Elijah Muhammad. He was always well dressed and was in all respects impressive in appearance. We rallied behind the brother.

Notice I don't mention his name. This is because in a short time he disgraced himself and in doing so nearly brought our community development to a halt. The problem was his behavior with women. At the time he was pulling us together as a community he was aggressively pursuing a Christian woman for marriage. To my knowledge his behavior was above board, but his interest was well known to many. When she showed signs of interest, community sisters, I among them, began to coach her about Islam and what she needed to know about being a Muslim woman, especially the wife of an imam.

She accepted Islam. The marriage took place. She proved herself to be a model Muslim and a model wife. For one, she became a very caring stepmother for the two teenage sons of the imam. The imam, on the other hand, proved himself to be less than a model Muslim and certainly less than a model leader. Not many months after his marriage there were rumors that he was having an affair. The rumors were substantiated. Under pressure from her relatives, his wife divorced him. She also left Islam. The community asked the minister to step down. He did.

Not too long before this occurrence, something similar happened to Thomas Shabazz in Jackson, Mississippi. I am not aware of the circumstances, but he was asked by his community to step down. He went to Chicago seeking to appeal but was not given an audience. He stepped down.

During the time the Inkster events were unfolding I heard from Thomas. He was back in Michigan. He wrote me seeking reconciliation. This was not good news. My life was hard, but I was making progress. I was attending college, pursuing a degree in Early Childhood Education. There was no place in my life for a man who was demanding and demeaning.

But I gave him an ear. I was raising his daughter and son. Maybe there could be for them the wholesome environment of a family with both parents present. Thomas seemed to hear and understand what I had to say about what was wrong with our first marriage. He seemed to understand that I would need him to be supportive so I could finish my degree, after which I could lend him the same support while he finished his. He seemed to be listening to and liking my vision. So, I agreed to remarry.

Dad did not say much, but he strongly disapproved. Mama was distraught and angry. She used very harsh words with me in expressing her disapproval. But I went ahead with the marriage. Thomas moved in with me and our children. Some of my friends, Muslim sisters, when they heard of it, they stopped speaking to me.

My parents and my friends were correct. The marriage lasted six months. Thomas left and did not contest the divorce.

Thomas had not been listening. He had not changed. In fact, he was worse. He was someone other than Minister Thomas Shabazz I married when I was nineteen. While that Thomas was not a caring husband, he clearly cared for and was dedicated to his principles. He was a man of his word. That was not the Thomas I remarried. I think he was one of several victims of the confusion in the Nation of Islam in the seventies.

CHAPTER TEN

ATLANTA

The seed for residing in Atlanta must have been planted in my head during the 60s. Honorable Elijah Muhammad had a special gathering for Muslims in Atlanta. My parents traveled there from Detroit to attend. Upon returning, they shared some of the things they observed. They were amazed to see the beautiful homes that some African Americans owned in Atlanta. There were many black people in prominent positions, especially women, even then. So, the time came for me to make my claim of going and being someplace that I had wanted to be for many, many years.

I had traveled back and forth from Detroit to Alabama, my birthplace, where I visited my grandparents and relatives. They all welcomed us and made us feel as comfortable and welcomed with whatever they had. Sometimes Dad would drive us from Michigan through parts of Ohio and Kentucky on to Alabama.

I appreciated the warm and beautiful spirit of the people, especially African Americans, who lived in Jackson, Mississippi. Living in Detroit did not move my soul as in the southern cities. Maybe there was something within me that longed for the time when I was a small girl in Bessemer, Alabama. One of my more significant concerns was the weather and how as a young girl, I had to trudge through the snow and ice, walking to and from the bus stop and having to bundle up like a teddy bear to keep warm. Sometimes I'd wear thermal long johns, two pairs of socks, boots, hats, and double-layered clothes trying to stay warm. Detroit just never was an ideal place in my mind. I did love the believers that made up our Muslim community. The close-knit association was reinforcing, especially how everyone would reach out and help one another whenever someone needed help.

I also appreciated that after Mama and Dad left the South, it seemed that one by one, family members moved from Alabama to Detroit or neighboring cities. They, too, were attracted to the North because there was more employment, especially in Detroit. Ford Motor Company and other auto companies offered a better way of life. There were more opportunities, even though people were still practicing racism in Detroit and other northern cities. However, Caucasians did not practice racism as overtly as they did in the south.

My Mama's younger brother, Obadiah (we called him Uncle Junior), worked for Ford Motor assembly in Romulus. He was a foreman for several years. As years passed, there did not seem to be as much progress for the black assembly-line workers as there should have been. This was the case throughout the United States. One of the last straws for me was when the major automobile plants closed, and the whole city and surrounding areas just seemed dead. There was blight and poverty everywhere. People had to struggle to eat and to keep a roof over their heads. I felt there just had to be something better than this.

Also, the masjid did not feel as welcoming as it had in the past. I guess everyone was feeling the pinch of the economy. Also, they were most likely feeling the changes that Imam W. Deen Muhammad had initiated in The World Community of Al-Islam, as the transformed Nation of Islam had come to be called. Some of the believers were slow to adapt to the changes.

Praise be to Allah, I began to discuss my plans for moving to Atlanta with my family, with the hope that they would be supportive. My family, especially my mother and father, we're resistant to my making a move. I had set the time for making the transition from Detroit to Atlanta for either the end of 1980 or the beginning of 1981. Some things were happening in Atlanta at the time that contributed to my parents feeling this way. From July 1979 through May of 1981, at least 28 black children went missing or were murdered in the Atlanta area. Atlanta authorities claimed it was Wayne Williams, a young black man about 25 years of age. This headline dominated the news that my mother and father got, so they objected to my moving to Atlanta at that time.

They asked me if I had thought the situation out before making my choice. I contacted some of the people I met while visiting Atlanta in 1979. I spoke with several sisters, and they assured me they would do all that they could to assist my children and me with accommodations and helping us to learn the city.

There was something I did do before making the arrangements for leaving Detroit. That was to check the job situation for elementary school teachers in Atlanta. I learned there would be a job fair in November of 1980, where principals would set up in a Community College auditorium in Macon, GA. Representatives from places all over Atlanta would be there taking applications and interviewing newly certified teachers. I felt this would be a suitable time for me to put my application in for work. I asked one of my sisters to keep my children for a couple of days. I obtained a rental car and drove to Macon, Georgia, for the job fair. I interviewed four principals from different parts of Georgia: from Fulton County, Clayton County, DeKalb County, and Harris County.

Picking up and going someplace without a permanent job and without having made living arrangements was not typical of me. However, I was so anxious to move that I didn't let anything stand in the way. I made a bold step in asking a family that I had only recently met when I'd visited Atlanta in 1978 if I could impose upon them to stay in their home for three to six weeks, myself and two children. They could have easily said no, as they did not know me; however, they said yes, and right away I began packing and arranging for the move. I contacted my brother James (who has always been a lifesaver), my brother-in-law Fareed Hasan, and my cousin Joseph Pacely. They agreed to assist me with moving.

January 1, 1981, we were on our way to Atlanta, Georgia. By this time my parents, with my siblings who were still at home, had relocated to San Diego, California. I bid farewell to family who were still in Inkster. I gave them the greetings and tried to give them assurance and put their minds at ease. I drove my 1976 Dodge Aspen station wagon with my two children, Yusuf and Aleisha. Joseph, my cousin, assisted me with driving. James and Fareed drove the U-Haul truck with my meager belongings.

My children and I were in our warmest and heaviest winter clothing: hats, mittens, gloves, boots, long johns, hats, scarves, layered and warm as protection from Michigan's cold weather. By the time we arrived in Tennessee, it was 67 degrees. We had begun pulling off some of the layers of clothing as we reached closer to our destination. By the time we reached Georgia, it was 70 degrees, and I couldn't believe that on January 1st it could be 70 degrees. I asked myself, "Where has this been all my life?!" Another contrast I noticed was the beautiful, plush green grass as we drove further south. And how clean the highways were! We didn't encounter a single pothole. We made a couple of stops. We stopped to refuel, and we stopped to get something to eat and drink.

We found storage for the things we brought from Detroit. Then we made it to the home of Iman and Wali Sabir. We spent a little time exchanging pleasantries and my helpers were soon on the road back to Detroit. Wali and Iman showed us our accommodations and made us feel welcomed. I thanked Allah for His mercies. We showered and went to bed.

The next day was Monday. Iman had to go to work, but I was welcomed to prepare breakfast for myself and the children. I began calling to set up interviews for substitute teaching and temporary clerical assignments. My only concern was what I would do about the children; I did not feel comfortable leaving them alone at someone's home while I worked. I asked Allah's guidance in dealing with this. My parents called to check on us and to see that we had made it safely. The next few days, the children and I drove around the immediate area, trying to become familiar with our new surroundings. After we were in Atlanta for two weeks, my parents asked if Yusuf could stay with them in California until I got settled. I thanked them and took them up on their offer to send an airline ticket for him. I was concerned about him traveling alone but felt that if I made sure he was on the flight and asked the stewardess to watch out for him, he would be okay. Yusuf made it safely to California; this was a relief. That left Aleisha and me. I enrolled Aleisha in school the next day.

I received another call from my mother and younger sister, Iatrice, who I hardly knew. I was in Jackson, Mississippi, when she was born and had very little time to get to know her upon returning to Detroit. She asked if she could come to Atlanta. I didn't mind her coming except that this was not the best time since I was not in my own place. She explained that Mama and Dad were not in the best mood for raising a teen and, besides, she wanted to get to know Aleisha better. Since my family had Yusuf, I felt it might work. I asked Iman and Wali, and they agreed. Between doing substitute teaching and temporary work (answering the telephone, filing, and light typing) I was able to get by. I offered Iman and Wali what I had. Iman suggested I keep what I was making and save it for getting my own apartment. It took me until March of 1981 to save enough money to have the first month's rent and security fee for an apartment. Brother Wali and another brother assisted me in moving to Tregoney East Apartments in Panthersville, about 30 minutes from Iman and Wali's home. We picked up the things I had left in storage.

I ended up selling the refrigerator and some of the other items. We stayed in Tregoney East Apartments for about six months before moving to Eastwick, off Candler Road near Highway 120.

By this time, I had been offered a teaching position with what is now Mohammed Schools of Atlanta. I would be replacing Wanda Sharieff, who was moving to El Paso, Texas. Imam Ibrahim Pasha led the interviewing process. I met the school Principal, Teresa Milwakkil and a school board member, Yusuf Milwakkil. I loved the atmosphere of the school. I was welcomed with open arms and felt very comfortable. My only question was, how will I maintain an apartment, feed my children and myself, have gas to go back and forth on the salary they offered. It was a real challenge.

I sent Iatrice back home to San Diego since she did not want to follow my rules and asked my parents to send Yusuf back so he could attend Mohammed Schools. Slowly but surely, I was beginning to make progress. I soon discovered I had some Muslim families as neighbors; many Muslim families chose to live in Eastwick during the eighties and nineties. One of the first families I met was Bayyinah Shaheed, who had recently moved from Oklahoma with her four children. There was Nabi and Jeanette Nu'man and their family. Jeanette was a teacher at Mohammed's school. Ibrahim Beyan, another Eastwick neighbor, also taught at Mohammed Schools. It made sense that the three of us would ride together to share the cost of gas. We did this for the two years I taught at Mohammed Schools.

There were others I met who made my early days in Atlanta most pleasurable. There was Brother Plemon El-Amin, who was an assistant imam to Imam Pasha. Imam Plemon later presided over the Atlanta Masjid for well over thirty years, before relinquishing his post to Imam Mansoor Sabree. Imam Mansoor after teaching for several years decided to do additional study of al-Islam and Arabic in Senegal. He passed his post over to Imam Suleiman Hamid and Imam Rashad. They are presently the imam and assistant imam of the Atlanta Masjid. Imam Plemon's daughter, Fatima El-Amin, was in my class along with many other young up and coming scholars, like Ruykiyyah Bilal, Suileman Wazeruddin, Aziz Khatib, Nasim Pasha (daughter of Imam Pasha), Zenobia Nabawi, Jamilah Karim, Shikery Muhyee, Rasheedah Saleem, and others.

I'm so grateful to Imam Plemon for sharing with me the proper way to perform salah. I had not learned to pray properly before coming to Atlanta. He shared other Islamic essentials with me and other teachers. The two years spent at Mohammed Schools were significant yet challenging. I am grateful that I was able to be a part of the school during this period.

My children and I made many sacrifices, as I'm sure most of the teachers there did. When I shared what we were experiencing with my family, my mother said, "Lynne, you know your father and I have sacrificed for our family. You have earned that piece of paper; now you go and do what you have to do to feed your family." Praise Be to Allah, for my mother! Always the voice of reason. I couldn't continue to teach at the school. I would have to seek employment elsewhere.

It was disheartening for me to leave the school. However, I had to make that choice. I was blessed to find work in a private school called Excelsior with an administrator who had taught in the public school system for almost twenty years. She employed certified elementary teachers to work in the Greenbriar area (at that time a well-to-do neighborhood in Atlanta). She had an outstanding program. Her emphasis was on teaching black history, math, and the arts to black children. The pay was comparable to that of public schools, but she could not afford to provide health benefits. I was able to stay with her for two school years before finally deciding to go to a public school.

I was happy that I chose to move to Atlanta. My experience reminds me of the movie Coming to America. Hakim, the main character, is so awe-struck by all he sees when he comes to America, he is willing to relinquish whatever he must to fit in, to feel a part of his new surroundings. I too was willing to help the school (and the masjid) despite the hardships and challenges. It was worth it.

I've met so many beautiful believers over the years. People like Khayriyyah Faiz, Mary Saleem, Lemumbah Faiz, Yusuf, Edwina Wazeerudin, Teresa Milwakkil, Mariam Shakir, Betty Hasan Amin. Ameedah, Booker Rashad Azizuddin, Waheedah Bilal, and others, many of which Allah has called. I'm so grateful that I chose to come to Atlanta!

APPENDIX

NATION OF ISLAM IN AMERICA: A NATION OF BEAUTY & PEACE

(copied and rendered verbatim from https:// www.noi.org/noi-history/)

On July the Fourth, the day of America's Independence celebration, He announced the beginning of His mission which was to restore and to resurrect His lost and found people, who were identified as the original members of the Tribe of Shabazz from the Lost Nation of Asia. The lost people of the original nation of African descent, were captured, exploited, and dehumanized to serve as servitude slaves of America for over three centuries. His mission was to teach the downtrodden and defenseless Black people a thorough Knowledge of God and of themselves, and to put them on the road to Self-Independence with a superior culture and higher civilization than they had previously experienced.

He taught us the ways of love and peace, of truth and beauty. We are being led into the path of a new spiritual culture and civilization of complete harmony and peace, one of refinement in the pursuit of happiness and eternal joy in the Supreme Knowledge of God and the Science of everything in life.

IN 1931, THE MASTER WAS preaching this Great Truth of salvation when He met a man named Elijah Poole in Detroit, Michigan. He chose him to be His Divine Representative in continuing this most difficult task of bringing truth and light to His lost and found people. For 3 1/2 years He taught and trained the Honorable Elijah Muhammad night and day into the profound Secret Wisdom of the Reality of God, which included the hidden knowledge of the original people who were the first founders of civilization of our Planet and who had a full knowledge of the Universal Order of Things from the beginning of the Divine Creation.

Upon the Master's departure in 1934, the Honorable Elijah Muhammad labored tirelessly to bring life to his mentally and spiritually dead people until his return to the Master in 1975. The Honorable Elijah Muhammad identified the Master as being the answer to the one that the world had been expecting for the past 2,000 years under the names Messiah, the second coming of Jesus, the Christ, Jehovah, God, and the Son of Man. When the Honorable Elijah Muhammad asked Him to identify Himself He replied that He was the Mahdi. He signed His name in 1933 as Master Wallace Fard Muhammad to express the meaning of One Who had come in the Early Morning Dawn of the New Millennium to lay the base for a New World Order of Peace and Righteousness on the foundation of Truth and Justice; to put down tyrants and to change the world into a Heaven on Earth.

During the Honorable Elijah Muhammad's initial 44 years, he suffered persecution & rejection from the very people whom he was appointed as a Servant of God. He was rejected and despised by the 10 percent leaders of America and the world because he revealed a Greater Truth and Wisdom that would end the old world of Satan's rule and dominion. He was not self-taught or self-made but ONE MIGHTY IN POWER had taught him what he knew not. The Honorable Elijah Muhammad had never received any more than a fourth grade education, yet his heart was true in what he saw and he saw the greatest of the Signs of his Lord.

The more converts that he made in the cities, in the by-ways, and in the highways of this land, along with receiving honor and fame abroad, the powerful leaders and rulers of this world grew in opposition. As the baby Nation of Islam came to birth in America, the world rulers were shaken in their foundation to learn of this miraculous achievement, and are today frustrated in plans to prevent our survival. The theme of the Holy Qur'an and Bible that most clearly defines this struggle is revealed in the history of Pharaoh's opposition to Moses and Aaron in the delivery of Israel in bondage in Egypt.

THE NATION OF ISLAM WAS founded on the basis of peace and as an answer to a prayer of Abraham to deliver his people who would be found in servitude slavery in the Western Hemisphere in this day and time. The Flag of Islam with the symbols of the Sun, Moon, and the Stars, represent the Universe and is also a Banner of Universal peace and Harmony. Our Holy Temples of Islam were established in America as sanctuaries of peace and higher learning into the Knowledge of the Oneness of God. Our schools are called Universities of Islam and teach the higher meaning of Islam which is Mathematics. We have always been taught to respect the laws of the land. We are taught never to carry arms, to make war or to be the aggressor, for this is against the nature of the righteous. We are taught the Principles of Divine Unity and the Universal Brotherhood of Islam.

We are taught cleanliness inwardly and outwardly with the practice of good manners and respect to one and all. We are taught that the family is the back bone of society and that our children must be reared to reflect the highest morals and training to perfect our society. We are trained to eat and to prepare the best of foods for the longevity of life, without the use of alcohol, smoking and substance abuse which endangers the ethics of healthy living. We are taught to respect and protect our women who are the mothers of civilization.

Our women are taught a dress code of modesty that will lead to the practice of high morality. We are trained to be an exemplary community expressing the highest spiritual goals for the reform of ourselves and others based on wisdom, knowledge and beauty.

Contrary to the inflammatory rhetoric that has been utilized by the news media and some community leaders to condemn the positive effects of Islam's influence in today's modern society, just the opposite is being proven true. The Nation of Islam (The Nation of Peace) represents hope to millions of our people in America and around the globe who have been deprived of the high standards of a righteous way of life.

This unity and love so sorely absent from our communities was genuinely exemplified by the millions of participants on the day of the Million Man March held in Washington, D.C., October 16, 1995. The exemplary Spiritual Leadership of Minister Louis Farrakhan in the rebuilding of the Nation of Islam in America is showing the way in the breaking down of barriers of communication throughout the society regardless to one's religious, racial, or ideological beliefs and views.

Through God's Divine Guidance, we are extending this Divine Work of moral and spiritual reform throughout the Western Hemisphere. God's Light and Truth will prevail against the darkness and falsehood of all opposition. In spite of the controversy and clamor surrounding the Nation of Islam and it's Divine Leader, Minister Louis Farrakhan, we are forging ahead in the Spirit of Almighty God, Allah, to unite with all of humanity in the Oneness of God, where all people of goodwill of every Race and of every Nation may participate in the Universal Expression of the Principles of Peace and the Brotherhood of man. This is the Beautiful Community of the Nation of Islam that is coming to birth in America on this Farthest Western Horizon in fulfillment of the Prophecy that God would meet with Muhammad for a second time and reveal to His servant What He Revealed. Thus the world is witnessing the Sun of Islam arising in the West. Praise the Holy Name of Allah, the Beneficent, the Merciful.

Where do we go from here in the remaining four years of the twentieth century? Will we continue to argue, to condemn, to fight and kill one another; or will we sit down and counsel with one another in seeking a just solution to the problems that beset us in

America and in the world? Wisdom decrees that in counsel and in dialogue is the way to peace. Foolishness decrees that if we ignore the warning signs, we will fall into the deeper abyss of Hell. God is the Judge today; and most surely upon Him do the Believers rely!

Document written by Minister, Writer, Music Composer and wife of the Honorable Elijah Muhammad
Mother Tynetta Muhammad
March 28, 1996

What follows addresses common and questions and misconceptions. The answers are from Honorable Elijah Muhammad. They come from him directly through two of his books: *How to Eat to Live* and *Message to the Blackman in America*. Indirectly they come from addresses collected at the website *www.studyal-islam.com*, addresses made by Muslims who experienced the Nation of Islam firsthand. Most answers are paraphrases rather than quotes.

QUESTIONS AND ANSWERS:

1. Did Muslims really eat one meal a day?

    Ans. The average believer ate one meal a day. Of course, this did not include children, pregnant women, and those that were ill. Honorable Elijah Muhammad says in *How to Eat to Live* that our biggest problem is eating too much and too often. He recommends eating once a day once every other day. This will take care of everything. You cannot go all over the earth trying to eat everything that people say is good to eat. But give what you do eat time to get out of the way for the next meal and the effect that probably would cause.

Brothers and sisters let your stomach rest. Stop trying to eat three meals a day, and all in between. That's enough to kill chickens and hogs. Yes, most Muslims changed their diets. You must not eat the swine meat, not any parts of it. Likewise, we were told not to drink alcohol. I can tell you unequivocally yes, that the majority of those that professed to follow the teachings ate one meal a day.

Many pioneer believers lived to be a ripe old age compared to what we see today. They did not suffer from many of the ailments that we see black people suffering from today, e.g., diabetes, hypertension, and obesity. Honorable Elijah Muhammad even recommended that we try eating every other day, or every 72 hours to keep strong and live a long, healthy life. Do not be frightened; eating one meal a day and the right foods at that one meal will help you eradicate much sickness and add years to your life.

2. Why did Honorable Elijah Muhammad encourage his followers to wear uniforms?

Ans. The purpose of uniforms was to bring forth the idea that uniformity of dress would encourage uniformity of heart and mind, thus, bring followers into one accord. Another purpose was to dispel jealousy and envy and encourage his people to be creative and design their own styles. This would also encourage believers to create jobs for one another.

"Every nation on earth has its own uniform." The uniform denotes unity and helps to distinguish Muslims from non-Muslims. Seeing a Fruit of Islam member, especially in uniform, made me know I would be protected in case something happened. I knew they were trained in security and martial arts. Members of Muslim Girls Training ("MGT") wore the same styles, but the colors distinguished the laborers and security personnel from the general membership. For example, for Savior's Day, you saw all MGT dressed in white. Sisters wore green or beige on other occasions. When we wore uniforms, we knew we were in accord with Islamic standards of dress.

3.   What was the economic blueprint of Honorable Elijah Muhammad?

Ans. He designed a five-year economic program for his people. It was not just for his followers but, rather, for black people. He suggested that black people put aside the monies they used for gambling, alcohol, cigarettes and other wasteful acts. That we should pool these resources by sending him as little as five cents a day or twenty-five cents a week. Within two to three years, we would accumulate a sizeable amount. We were to acknowledge and recognize that we are members of the Creator's "nation" and that we should act accordingly. This action required Muslims to set an example for the "lost-found" people in the "Wilderness of North America." This required actions and deeds, not lip service! He offered the following five points as a blueprint for success:

- Recognize the necessity for unity and group operation (i.e., action).
- Pool resources, physical and financial.
- Stop wanton criticism of everything black owned and black operated.
- Keep in mind that jealousy destroys from within.

- Observe the operations of the white man. He is successful. He makes no excuses for his failures. He works hard in a collective manner.

If there are six or eight Muslims with the knowledge or experience of the grocery business, pool your knowledge and open a grocery store. If there are those with knowledge of dressmaking, merchandising, trade, maintenance—pool your knowledge. Do not be ashamed to seek knowledge and assistance from the brother or sister who has more knowledge and training than you. Work together and seek Allah's Guidance.

4. Were Muslims discouraged from obtaining a formal education?

Some officials were known to discourage younger followers from furthering their education. They would say, "A Muslim doesn't need a white man's education." But those same officials were known to find placement for brothers and sisters who came with Elementary and Secondary Education backgrounds, or bookkeeping and accounting knowledge, or higher math skills. Those officials would always publicly acknowledge doctors, engineers, and nurses. When believers posed the question to the Honorable Elijah Muhammad, his answer was that we should strive to obtain an education and get an education that could be used for the benefit of our people. He preferred that sisters not live on college campuses, that they commute from home rather than live on campus.

5.   What did it mean to be put in Class C or Class F?

Ans. Ostracism. If a believer was put into Class C, it meant that he/she was given time away from the General Membership because they had broken a rule. The rules were in two categories:

Class C: For a first time Class C infraction a believer was given from 30 to 60 days. Violators were allowed to attend temple meetings but could not associate with other believers. Class C infractions included things like drinking alcohol, smoking cigarettes, smoking marijuana, deliberately speeding on the highway, lying, gambling, frequenting places Muslims should not frequent (e.g., night clubs).

Class F: Being found guilty of an offense that could carry a penalty of 90 days or more. Infractions included things like adultery/fornication, fighting one another, and disobeying orders, especially those issued by Honorable Elijah Muhammad.

Those who were sincere and had made mistakes were anxious to fulfill the punishment and get back in good standing. Some believers were lost due to the tone that was set by those in charge. Others were lost because expectations had not been clearly communicated to them.

6.   How effective was the dawah of NOI in awakening the "mentally dead" (i.e., non-Muslims)

Ans. The most effective dawah effort of NOI was the newspaper *Muhammad Speaks*. It reached a peak circulation of 1.2 million in the early '70s, becoming the nation's largest African-American weekly. Every issue Included an article conveying the teachings of Honorable Elijah Muhammad. In his best-seller, *The Fire Next Time*, James Baldwin wrote of Honorable Elijah Muhammad that he had been able to do what generations of welfare workers, committees, and housing projects had failed to do, namely heal and redeem drunkards and drug addicts as well as divert people from prison and reform the formerly incarcerated.

7.   What was it about the Nation of Islam that attracted the "so-called Negro" During the '60s and '70s?

Ans. People were seeing the changes being made by the followers Honorable Elijah Muhammad. Many had relatives that had been in the penile system and could see the positive changes they were making in their lives. He rekindled a sense of self-pride, self-esteem, cultural awareness in people. He encouraged them to clean themselves up from alcohol, drugs, permissiveness, and other ills. He demonstrated how to pool their resources, enabling them to invest in business, farmland, grocery stores, and banks. Many charged that what he taught was not religion but social reform. The answer to that charge is that the results were both useful and beneficial to the soul.

8.   Did Honorable Elijah Muhammad teach hate?

Ans. No. But he gave those accusers a dose of their own medicine. During the early years of his mission, Honorable Elijah Muhammad often cited the 400-year history of lynchings and Jim Crow. "They say I'm a teacher of racial hatred. Caucasians don't like to hear the truth, especially when it's against them. It's a terrible thing for such people to charge me with teaching hatred when their feet are on my people's neck. They tell us to our faces that they hate black people. We must not hate them for hating you."

Honorable Elijah Muhammad taught his people to love themselves first. "You must have a love for self and kind." "Self-reliance is the key."

"One of the gravest handicaps among the so-called Negroes is that there is no love for self nor love for his/ her own kind. Not having love for self is the root cause of hate (dislike), disunity, disagreement, quarreling, betraying, being a stool pigeon, and fighting and killing one another. How can you be loved if you have not love for self and your own nation, and dislike being a member of your own? Then what nation will trust your love and membership?" Honorable Elijah Muhammad often quoted Marcus Garvey (i.e., Honorable Marcus Mosiah Garvey): "Up You Mighty Nation. You Can Accomplish What You Will!"

THINKING OF MOMMA

Momma would have turned 96 on July 4, 2021. Momma, Sister Irene, Sister Muhsinah, Mother Irene and Mother Muhsinah as she was referred to, was truly a one-of-a-kind individual. She was a "best friend," to each of her 11 children, and truly a blessing to all the people whose lives she touched.

Momma read to us and recited poetry she knew verbatim from the great poets such as, Langston Hughes, Paul Lawrence Dunbar, Gwendolyn Brooks, Richard Wright, James Weldon Johnson, William Wordsworth, Walt Whitman, T.S. Eliot, Alfred Lloyd Tennyson, Emily Dickenson, and Charles Dickens, just to name a few. As a result of teaching us we became good readers.

Momma recognized in each of us our special gifts and strengths that God placed in us and was able to nurture those gifts. Momma was able to give us tools in which to navigate through this world. She along with my father taught us to value ourselves, to value others, she appreciated and encouraged our curiosity, and self-expression, and taught us self-discipline.

Momma taught us to always use the good manners that she and my father taught us. They taught us to use our good manners at home and abroad.

Momma taught us "Life Lessons," from the Bible and the Quran. My mother grew up in the Holiness Church, since her mother,

Grandma Nancy Pacely was a member of the Holiness church in Bessemer, Alabama. Momma was proficient in the Bible and later became adept in the Quran once she became a member of the Nation of Islam and started studying the Quran.

She taught us about being honest, trustworthy, kind, about sharing with people who are less fortunate, about being considerate of others, and about being patient and tolerant.

Momma was devoted to the teachings of the Honorable Elijah Muhammad and also a very open and broadminded person. Momma was truly a seeker of knowledge and had friendships in all walks of life. Momma truly sought knowledge from the "Cradle to the Grave."

One thing that was very notable about momma is that she was always surrounded by books. She was an avid student of everything positive. She loved studying herbs and about nature's cures. She also studied social sciences and psychology and was always keeping abreast of the latest parenting skills.

Momma was a prayer warrior, a naturopath without documentation, a wonderful mother who knew how to hug and to make our life fun and disciplined at the same time. One very important thing about momma, she really knew how to laugh, she would laugh to the point of tears.

In the early 1960's after having about seven children, Momma went to night school to learn bookkeeping in order to help our father in his construction company. Her formal education included attending Miles College in Alabama for two years after high school and receiving an associates degree in Childhood Development from Wayne County Community College in Michigan in 1977.

Our mother was ahead of her time in terms of recycling. She recycled everything and since she was a child who grew up during the Great Depression, she was very conscious of not wasting food, clothing, or anything. Since she and my father planted a garden each year, momma canned the fresh vegetables and fruits from the garden. In terms of clothing, after they had been handed down and handed around she would cut them into square or other shapes and use them for quilts. One of her favorite sayings was "waste not, want not."

All of our meals were prepared from scratch with lots of love. Momma was an excellent baker and cook. When she baked whole yeast bread when could smell it from the corner as we were getting off the school bus, and so did everyone else on Henry Street. Momma would always make enough to share with the neighborhood children as they would come and knock on the door and ask for it. These same children would tease us about being the bean soup family.

If I had to pick three outstanding things about momma they would be: Her faith and belief in Allah and the power of prayer: Her love and commitment to her family which included her nuclear family as well as her extended family: and her thirst to always read, listen and learn. She was an eternal student.

My mother and father made great sacrifices to send the first four children (Lynice, James, Jonathan, and Renee) to the Muslim school which was The University of Islam. Because momma and our father showered us with a strong sense of self and unconditional Love, we grew up with a very positive sense of self-worth.

Because my mother and father were such dynamic duo, they worked together to always make sure that we had the best that they could provide for us.

REMEMBERING
A REMARKABLE MAN

This man survived an ore mine explosion in Alabama in the early 1940s. The ore mine explosion left him nearly dead. He shared with us that he was in the morgue, and he heard the attendants getting ready to embalm him. He said he heard them talking and one of the attendants held a mirror to his nose and saw that he was still breathing so they took measures to revive him and save his life.

This remarkable man that I speak of was my father, born James Emerson Robinson, Robinson was his stepfather's name, his birth father's name was Harvey Jordan. He was born on August 29, 1920, in Hale County, Alabama to Queen Jones and Harvey Jordan. My Grandfather Harvey Jordan was married to another lady given to him by an Indian tribe as a gift. My father and his sister Mary Robinson were always welcomed in his birthfather's home and always treated well by his birth father's wife and children.

I thank Allah for sparing my father's life. Had it not been for that blessing from Allah, my father would not have met and married my mother in 1945 and not any of the eleven children that they had together would have been born. Alhamdulillah for that blessing.

As a member of the Nation of Islam, my father was known as Brother James E. 5 X of Inkster, Michigan, and during the time that Imam Warith Deen Muhammad begin to transition the Nation of Islam to follow the Sunnah of Prophet Mohammed, my father changed his name to Suleiman Bilal.

My parents married in June of 1945; my father had purchased a house in Bessemer, Alabama before marrying my mother, (Ireana Costella Pacely). My three older siblings, Lynice, James, and Jonathan were born in Bessemer, Alabama.

My parents sold their house and moved to Detroit, Michigan in 1951 where my father became a member of the Nation of Islam. I was born in June of that year.

As a member of the Nation of Islam, my father managed and worked one of the first farms that the Honorable Elijah purchased. It was located in White Clouds, Michigan. My father would travel from White Clouds, to Chicago, Illinois bi-monthly to report directly to the Honorable Elijah regarding the farm. My father was also one of the special F.O.I (Fruit of Islam) security team to the Honorable Elijah Muhammad.

My parents were ardent supporters of the University of Islam in Detroit, Michigan. Where my older brothers and sister, and I attended until we had to start attending public school in Inkster, Michigan.

My father was a brick mason by trade and was educated in agricultural science at Tuskegee Institute. In the early 1950s, my father started his own construction company, James E. Robinson and Son's Construction company. My father along with my Uncle Johnny George one of his brothers-in-law and my father's work crews built manholes, catch basins, and sewage systems for many of the subdivisions in the suburbs of 1960s.

His construction company laid the foundations for many of the subdivisions that were built in many of the suburbs and cities in Michigan in the 1960s and '70s, places such as Adrian, Allen Park, Birmingham, Farmington Hills, Lincoln Park, Northville, Rochester, Royal Oak, and St. Claire Shores. Brother Malcolm worked on one of my father's work crews for a very short period of time, as my father put it, he just was not cut out for that type of work. Yes, this is the same man that the world knows as Malcolm X. However, Brother Malcolm did excel at selling Stanley Home Products mentored by my mother, Sister Irene.

My father taught us African American history as well as American and world history. He also taught us about art, poetry, and to encourage us to read and investigate events on our own, he invested in a set of Encyclopedia Britannica and Child Craft books which had various stories, arts and crafts, and activities to challenge us.

Although my father worked very hard to support us, he valued spending special time with us as a family. He took time out each year to take the whole family on a vacation to Alabama where we would spend time with his family and friends as well as the mother's family and friends. We would go to the Michigan State Fair each year and as well as participating in a Pic-Nic in the park with the Pacelys, my mother's side of the family each year.

My father was a man of very distinctive and distinguished taste.

My father took such pride in providing the best for his family, we always got new clothes at the beginning of winter and summer. I remember when my father bought each one of us a brand-new bike and they were the top-of-the-line bikes, Schwinns.

My father taught us by example, to be honest, helping others, being respectful and considerate of others, sticking up for each other as siblings.

He taught us to always have good manners at home and abroad. The values that he and my mother taught us have benefitted us throughout our lives.

To me, my father was a giant among men, although he only stood 5ft. 4 inches.

My father James E. 5 X, Suleiman Bilal, was truly a remarkable man to have achieved and accomplished the things that he did during a time when this country was and still is very outwardly racist.

My father was a very charitable, compassionate, intelligent man who was wise enough to choose a woman, my mother as a wonderful helpmate. Our parents taught us to always carry ourselves in a dignified manner and to be intelligent and respectful.

One of the things that our father taught us is "there is good in the worst of us and bad in the best of us, and it is up to God to judge the rest of us." In other words, as we know a Muslims. Allah is the best of judges.

SAYINGS FROM MOM & DAD

Proverbs-Steel sharpens steel, men sharpen one another-
Just wait until you're in your birthday suit, I'm going to pay you up for old and new!

To you be your way, and to me be mine!
An apple a day, keeps the doctors away!
It's all in divine order!
Look, I brought you in this world, and I'll take you out of it!
A bird in hand is worth more than two in the bush!
Mama would say: You don't have a pot to piss in, nor a window to throw it out of!
Give me my roses while I'm here! Mom told us, especially in her later years, don't buy me any greeting cards and sentiments, write to me from your heart!

"A good name is better than gold"!
My word is my bond, and bond is life, I will give my life before my word shall fail.
An ounce of prevention is worth a pound of cure!
A penny saved, is a penny earned!
Waste not, want not!
Birds of the feather stick together!

Go forward and let your light shine!
Be an example of what you teach!
Be careful about the company you keep it may come back to haunt you!
Do unto others as you would have them do unto you!

BISMILLAH
JAMES MUHAMMAD

My name is James Muhammad, formerly James Emerson Robinson. I am the second child and oldest son born to James and Irene Pacely Robinson. My parents later adopted the names Suleiman and Muhsinah Bilal. I was born October 25, 1948, in Bessemer, Alabama. From the time I was 12, I worked with my father in his construction company. I graduated from Inkster High School in Inkster, Michigan in 1966. While attending Inkster High, I was a member of the wrestling, track, tennis, and swimming teams.

After high school, I attended Washtenaw Community College located in Ypsilanti, Michigan. In 1969 I left Michigan to attend Hampton Institute, now known as Hampton University, located in Hampton, Virginia. Hampton University is one of the Historically Black Colleges and Universities (HBCUs). I received a professional degree in Architectural Engineering in 1973.

I returned to Michigan and worked for several architectural firms in the Detroit metropolitan area. Early in my career, I was offered a position at General Motors Corporation. At General Motors I worked in the Estimating, Design and Facilities departments. During my employment with GM, I worked on a variety of projects at many of the GM sites and was able to travel extensively throughout the United States. In 2008 I retired from General Motors, after 29 years of employment,

I met Linda Robinson while attending Hampton Institute. We married in 1973 and had three daughters, Aliya, Tasja, and Sakinah (who passed away in 2020). We are now blessed to have six grandchildren: Derrick, Amani, Aquan, Ashaine, Ameron and Anissah. They are the joy of our lives.

There are two memorable experiences I would like to share. When I was about 5, my father managed the Nation of Islam farm in White Clouds, Michigan. My father had the responsibility of reporting the progress of the farm to Honorable Elijah Muhammad. I accompanied my father on the three-hour trips to Chicago for meetings. We met at the home of Honorable Elijah Muhammad. We removed our shoes as we entered the large palatial home. While waiting for the conclusion of their meeting, I let my feet sink into the elegant carpeting. I was intrigued as I looked around the room at the beautiful pictures on the walls and as I looked up at the sparkling chandelier hanging from the high ceiling. At the conclusion of a meeting, Honorable Elijah Muhamad would invite us to join him for his evening meal before we started on our journey back home. On several occasions, Honorable Elijah Muhammad asked my father if I could stay and spend time with him.

The second experience occurred while I was still a young boy living in White Clouds. From the teachings of the Honorable Elijah Muhammad, I had learned of the existence of large flying objects which scientists at that time referred to as Unidentified Flying Objects (UFOs). One day while outside with my brother, Jonathan, I saw what looked like a flying object in the sky, but it did not look like an airplane. It hovered overhead in the sky for a short while, and then it made quick moves to the left and to the right. Then after changing its trajectory, it began moving in an upward and downward motion. I realized this object was not an airplane because it was not possible for an airplane to move in that manner. I stood mesmerized as I continued to watch this object in the sky, glistening in the sunlight, when it suddenly vanished out of sight. Both memorable experiences made an indelible impression on me.

JONATHAN ROBINSON/JONATHAN RAHEEM MUHAMMAD

JANUARY 2, 1950 – MARCH 20, 2015

Jonathan was born in Bessemer, Alabama. He was the third of eleven children born to James E. 5 X Robinson and Irene X Robinson. Jonathan graduated from Inkster High school in 1968. He was a member of the track, tennis, and wrestling teams. He was an outstanding math student and never backed down from a good debate in and away from school.

Against the advice of his parents and siblings, Jonathan joined the Marines upon completing high school. However, pneumonia he'd suffered as a child resurfaced after serving a little more than a year. Jonathan received a physical disability discharge.

Jonathan and his brother James were news carriers, delivering Detroit News and Detroit Free Press to hundreds of well-satisfied customers over the years. He also worked with our father and uncle Johnny on many construction projects. He became a master welder and worked as a tree cutter and tractor trailer driver before serving in the Marines.

Jonathan was a member of the Nation of Islam, where he took an active part in advocating for the rights of our people and seeking redress of the injustices suffered by them. He was an ardent supporter and follower of the teachings of the Nation of Islam as taught by Honorable Elijah Muhammad and, later, Minister Louis Farrakhan.

Jonathan was married twice. In his first marriage, to Mary Smith, he fathered three children: Sakinah Robinson, Jonathan Robinson Jr., and Rasheedah Robinson. At the time of his transition, in 2015, Jonathan was married to Deborah, a wonderful stepmother for the three.

RENEE'S AUTOBIOGRAPHY

My name is Renee Ziyadah Hasan, my name at birth was Renee Robinson. I was the fourth child and second daughter of eleven children born to James Emerson Robinson and Irene (Pacely) Robinson. My father later adopted the name Suleiman Bilal, and my mother adopted the name, Muhsinah Bilal. After marrying William Howard Haywood, my name was Renee Haywood, until we decided to change our name legally to William Fareed Hasan, and to Renee Ziyadah Hasan.

I was born on June 6, 1951, in Detroit, Michigan. I attended the University of Islam in Detroit, Michigan from age 3 until I started Douglas Elementary public school in Inkster, Michigan when I was in the 5th grade, because we no longer had viable transportation to and from the University of Islam in Detroit.

I graduated from Inkster High School in 1968, attended Washtenaw Community College and received an associates degree in Food Technology. I then attended Tuskegee Institute for one semester in the fall of 1970 after which time I returned to Michigan and attended Eastern Michigan University where I received a bachelors degree in December of 1976 in Consumer Education and continued to receive my masters degree in Consumer Education in 1979.

I have always been loud and obnoxious, fun loving, very talkative, friendly, and extremely curious. Being bought up in the Nation of Islam taught me to be disciplined, reliable, generous, thoughtful, fair, patient, firm, reflective and purposeful. Sisters learned in the MGT and GCC, (Muslim Girls Training and General Civilization Classes) Muslim sisters should not be loud and vociferous in public.

I have learned to put Allah first always and family next. My family has always been my secure and safe haven. I have always valued my family life highly. My parents gave us a sense of security by providing us with food, clothing, shelter and more than that, they gave us a real sense of loving and belonging.

I am most grateful to Allah for blessing me to have witnessed the manner in which our parents raised us to be responsible, respectful, and God-fearing, and how they worked together as a team. I appreciate the fact that my parents were able to talk to us and give us tools and direct our path in life to be productive individuals.

I am grateful to Allah that I was blessed to marry a man who fully embraced the teachings of the Nation of Islam and then embraced Al-Islam once Imam Warith Deen Muhammad directed the community towards the Sunnah of Prophet Mohammed (PBUH).

Praise be to Allah, my husband and I raised three children, two males and one female, who are independent thinkers and who are developing businesses and programs that are benefitting them and other blacks as well as humanity.

William transitioned from this life to return to Allah in 2011, May Allah forgive him his sins and grant him Jennah. We have from our three children eleven grandchildren and two great-grandchildren, alhamdulillah.

I thank for blessing me to have worked with children for most of my professional life, as a substitute teacher, as a principal of a Sister Clara Muhammad school and as Child Protective Services Specialist for Children's Protective Services in Houston, Texas. The last experience that I had working with children was teaching English as a second language to students at an English Academy in Daegu, South Korea.

NANCY MARIE ROBINSON AKA SAKEENAH SABREE CALDWELL AKA MOMMY SAKEENAH!

Sakeenah was born May 9, 1955, in Inkster, Michigan. She was the sixth of eleven children born to James E. 5 X Robinson and Irene X Robinson. Sakeenah was educated at the University of Islam in Detroit, MI, and graduated in 1972.

Sakeenah was the mother of nine children. Seven from her first marriage and two from her second marriage: Nadiyah Pierre, Nura Caldwell, Sulieman Caldwell, Zenobia Caldwell, Ahmad Caldwell, Laila Caldwell, Salahudeen Caldwell, Shareefah (Ahmadna) Abdul-Qadir, and Rahamatullah Abdul-Qadir. Sakeenah has twelve grandchildren. Sakeenah is known for her patience, kindness, non-judgmental attitude towards others. In addition to her loving, nurturing spirit, mama Sakeenah was one of the gentlest and peaceful persons you would ever want to meet.

Sakeenah was a member of the Nation of Islam, and my memory of my mother in the nation was at the age of six years old, watching her make delicious homemade cakes, pies, ice-cream (Famous Bean Ice-Cream) and of course her famous Bean soup. My family was devout followers of Elijah Muhammad the nation, and quite naturally, my family perfected the bean pie and bean soup recipes. I have very fond memories of waking up to homemade Cinnamon Rolls, Fresh Bread with butter on the side! A large pot of bean soup for lunch! Hence the need for fresh bread and butter on the side.

My mother and grandfather would make fresh bean soup, and bake fresh bread, & bean pies to sell at Sunday morning temple services.

Mama was an excellent seamstress. She would design beautiful garments for herself, her daughters, her sisters and grandma. She was able to look at a pattern and adapt it to fit the person.

Sakeenah truly believed in the principles of the Nation of Islam, unity, self-help, discipline, and maintaining a healthy diet with putting only the best foods in your system.

BENITA BILAL TONEY/ AKA BENITA ROBINSON

AUGUST 19, 1959 – OCTOBER 10, 2010

B enita Bilal Toney was born August 19, 1959, in Wayne County Michigan to Suleiman Bilal (James E. Robinson) and Muhsinah Irene Bilal (Irene Pacely). She was the fraternal twin of Bernard Robinson. * Benita was the fifth daughter of eleven children (five boys and six girls).

Benita was educated at the University of Islam in Detroit, Michigan, as well as in Inkster Public Schools. In the seventies she moved to San Diego, California, where she studied to be a flight attendant. While working as a flight attendant she met James Edward Toney. They married August 19, 1979. James encouraged her to continue her career. Benita decided against this because it would keep her away from her family. She and James were blessed with four children, three daughters and one son: Kyresha Marie, Janae Patrice, Sirrese Danielle, and Aaron Ishmael.

Benita later attended Pacific College of Medical and Dental Assistants in San Diego. She graduated in 1982. She excelled as a dental assistant, and after working for a short time she became an administrative assistant. Soon after, she assumed the position of office manager, a role she filled for twenty-five years.

Benita was a devoted wife and mother. She was a wonderful example of kindness, tempered with love, generosity, and a loving spirit. She rendered service with love and compassion, always without judgment.

---

*Bernard Robinson, Benita's fraternal twin, made his transition on December 3, 1991. He died at 32 years of age. Heart trauma due to drugs. They both attended U.O.I. as well as Inkster Public Schools.

IATRICE IRENA GUERRERO

AKA Baby I.I., now commonly known as Lita, was born February 15, 1968, to Irene and James Robinson. They were shocked and elated to know that the 11th child, 6th daughter, was on the way while they were planning the wedding of their first born, Lynice. Iatrice grew up with the benefit of having her parents and grandparents rolled up into one, since they were in their mid-forties (Irene) and early fifties (James) when they had her.

Her first school was the University of Islam Temple No.1. where she learned not only reading, writing, and arithmetic, but also The Actual Facts, General Orders, English Lesson Number C1, and Quranic Scriptures. After the departure of Honorable Elijah Muhammad in 1976 and the closure of all the UOI's, she attended a series of schools and colleges throughout her life, but none ever equaled UOI. She moved to Atlanta her senior year of High School to establish residency to avoid out of state fees in order to attend a HBCU, a trick she learned from her older siblings.

After attending Georgia State University, Iatrice worked in corporate America with companies such as AT&T, Sprint, and Coca-Cola USA. Finding little satisfaction with making these companies richer, working on the "Corporate Plantations," she decided to work for herself, using all she had learned while working for various corporations and for her parents, both entrepreneurs. For two decades she and her husband, Nicolas James Guerrero, ran a successful Point of Sales company, Merchant Solutions, until the market crash in 2007.

Iatrice was diagnosed with Multiple Sclerosis in 1995, just a year after marrying Nicolas. A year a later they were blessed with their first child, a son, Rasulullah Jamal. Eleven years later, in 2007, their daughter Soledad Laxmi was born. She refers to Soledad as "the light and joy of my life."

Iatrice and Nicolas are the survivors of a near fatal car accident in 2018. After healing from two broken legs (having to learn to walk again), Iatrice is now retired and enjoys taking care of the Love of her Life (Nicolas), the Joy of her Life (Soledad), and the "Hope of her Life" (her grandson Miguiel Omari). Always wishing and praying for the best that life offers for my son and first born Rasul. Iatrice, through Allah's Grace and Mercy, continues beating the odds.

SOME FAMILY PHOTOGRAPHS

Left to right: Obie, Renee, Jonathan, James, Lynice

With my sisters

Dutiful FOI, my brothers (left to right): Harvey, Obie, Jonathan, James

My daughter Aleisha at age 12, shortly before our moving to Atlanta

Mama with five of her six sisters. California, 1977

James with his wife and three daughters

Mama holding Renee's oldest son Ihsan Jomo Hasan

Obie, Renee, Jonathan, James, Lynice holding Baby Sakinah

*Dad walking me down the isle. LeMoyne
Gardens; Inkster, Michigan; 1967*

With Aleisha and Yusuf in Jackson, Mississippi

With Aleisha and Yusuf in Atlanta, Georgia

Dad, Mama, Lynice, Thomas, Mama Nettie

*With Sister Shafeeqah at a teachers conference
in Sedalia, North Carolina*

*Aleisha and Yusuf promoting _Muhammad
Speaks_, Jackson, Mississippi*

With five grandchildren, 2001

Mama on a visit to Atlanta prior to moving there

Lynice and Renee, 2010

Bernard, twin to Benita Bilal Toney

SOURCES CONSULTED

C. Eric Lincoln. *The Black Muslims in America.* (Boston: Beacon Press, 1961).

Dawn-Marie Gibson, Jamilah Karim. *Women of the Nation: Between Black Protest and Sunni Islam.*

Elijah Muhammad. *History of the Nation of Islam.* (Published posthumously, Copyright 1993.)

Elijah Muhammad. *How To Eat to Live.*

Elijah Muhammad. *Message to The Blackman in America.*

Elijah Muhammad. "Be Yourself and Do Something for Self." *Muhammad Speaks,* July 4, 1969.

StudyAl-Islam.com. *Study Al-Islam Presents an Academic Examination of Elijah Muhammad's Contribution to the Ministry of Imam W. D. Mohammed.* Zaytuna College, Berkley, California. October 27, 2018.

ABOUT THE AUTHOR

Lynice Muhammad is a retired elementary teacher, mother, grandmother, and great-grandmother.

She is a second-generation Muslim dedicated to tracing her parents' legacy, as well as that of pioneer Muslim Believers, from the early 1950s.

Lynice is the eldest of eleven children and was depended upon to set the example for her younger siblings. She wants others to realize how sincere, loving and caring the pioneer believers were. Their genuine sharing helped set the stage for youth and younger believers to be motivated and inspired to become active participants of the N.O.I.

Lynice has a degree in Elementary Education, from Madonna University, located in Livonia, MI. She earned a Master of Arts degree from Cambridge University in Elementary Education, from Cambridge, Mass.

In addition to thirty years of teaching experience both as an Islamic and public school educator, she was an executive director of a home that provided a safe place for teen mothers and their babies. The task was to assist young girls and their babies and to offer them a chance to better prepare for their future.

Lynice is at her best with people and is actively involved with Toastmasters, where she was awarded the DTM (Distinguished Toastmaster), the highest award given to a Toastmaster. She is an active member of SUIH for over twenty years.

An organization of Muslim women working with the homeless and other worthwhile projects.

Her book, My Journey Through The Nation of Islam focuses on the journey she experiences from childhood to becoming a young woman and growing up in the Nation of Islam.

She may be contacted at *lynicem@yahoo.com.*

Lightning Source UK Ltd.
Milton Keynes UK
UKHW010657231221
396095UK00001B/172